DAILY PUT ON THE WHOLE ARMOR OF GOD

"Dress for Spiritual warfare."

TERESA S. MCCURRY

Printed in the United States of America

First Printing, April 2021

ISBN: 978-1-7338770-5-3

MCCURRY MINISTRIES INTERNATIONAL

DAILY PUT ON THE WHOLE ARMOR OF GOD

CONTENTS

Foreword

Pastor Tee has Masterfully unpacked The total Armour of God. I have had the opportunity to watch over the last ten years, the prophetic word of God being demonstrated in her life. You too will experience this prophetic flow which pours out through her writing and the power of her detailed teaching will show you how to access the deeper things of God through prayer. She skillfully teaches us that "That the word of God is a discerner of your thoughts and the intent of your heart." (Chapter 6) This Call to Action book instructs us to be proactive when a Prophetic word is given to us, this level of Obedience assures manifestation in our lifes. (Luke 1:38 Let it be to me according to your word.) Your Spirit man will come to life, your mind awaken as you enter into this dressing room. Strategically planning how to put on our daily armour. It reminds me of how David was offered King Saul's armour and why he refused the king's offer. He stated he had not proved and work with the King's armour before so he wasn't comfortable wearing it, However, he had dressed himself daily in the king of Kings armour and he knew and understood how to maneuver in it. Picture a young lady wearing her Mother high heel shoes, she's not stable in them. She is wobbling all around and tripping over her feet. This is because they are not her shoes, but as she grows and get her own pair of high heel shoes, well then, she's ready to slay. You too will be ready to slay the enemy after experiencing the spiritual insight of the two invisible kingdoms. The riveting revelation that Pastor Teresa shares gives us the warning that we must understand what's currently and constantly going on in these two realms. You must be aware. And understand the difference between the two. It's like a woman having on a Black dress is a different Motive and Spirit then a woman putting on "The Little Black Dress" Many people are underdressed for the spiritual situation that they are in. Throughout this book you will learn how to properly apply each article of the Armour of God to your daily routine, to assure that you are totally covered as you walk along your spiritual journey. Before leaving out of the door, The Whole Armour is required. Don't leave home without.

God Bless you Pastor Teresa as you continue to write, teach and translate the word of God that transforms the hearts of men. I love you.

Apostle, Dr. Arcenia Finley Founder of H.2O.
His to Obey Global Alliance Ministries.

INTRODUCTION

Now that we are in quarantine, I have more than enough time to complete the books God has placed on my heart, I am pleased to be writing to you during these difficult times. I started writing this project some time back, and this is based on my teachings from my Sunday morning sermons. I see God's hand at work in the midst of spiritual warfare, just what this book is all about. I have been in the ministry for ten years now, have enjoyed the ride, yet have realized that there are essential things that we must master to become a stable child of God through and through.

I was completing this book during this challenging time of Coronavirus [COVID -19] has shown me that above everything else, we need God's protection, and we must be in the right standing with Him, always. As such, it makes the message of this series, I taught about being dressed for battle , the ultimate weapon of prayer and the promises of God in him are Yes and Amen. this trilogy series is SOOOO relevant for the season we are in. In this series, I have started with showing us that we need to put on the whole armor of God for everything else to follow just in line with Gods word.

Following Christ is a journey, and it comes with its own processes, which we as belivere , face several opposing forces, by which we need to react and stay safe from their claws. In this book, teaching about the whole armor of God has given me so much pleasure, as it teaches on what puts you at a better position of understanding that God is fighting off the devil and his trickery on our behalf. In other words, we must put on the armor of God as it is your only protection from the enemy as we FIGHT THE GOOD FIGHT OF FAITH.

As a pastor, I desire to see the children of God live their lives with GREATER UNDERSTANDING. For this reason, I wish you to take this book seriously, and make sure also to get the next two books of this series.

CHAPTER ONE

Helmet Of Salvation

The Whole Armor of God

[10] finally, my brethren, be strong in the Lord and the power of His might. [11] Put on the whole armor of God that you may be able to stand against the wiles of the devil. [12] For we do not wrestle against flesh and blood, but against principalities, against powers, against the rulers of the darkness of this age, against spiritual hosts of wickedness in the heavenly places. [13] Therefore take up the whole armor of God that you may be able to withstand in the evil day, and having done all, to stand. [14] Stand, therefore, having girded your waist with truth, having put on the breastplate of righteousness.

¹⁵ and having shod your feet with the preparation of the gospel of peace. ¹⁶ above all, taking the shield of faith with which you will be able to quench all the fiery darts of the wicked one. ¹⁷ And take the helmet of salvation, and the sword of the Spirit, which is the word of God ¹⁸ always praying with all prayer and supplication in the Spirit, being watchful to this end with all perseverance and supplication for all the saints
— (Ephesians 6:10-18).

THIS IS THE FIRST book of a trilogy series. I named this first one, Daily Put on the whole armor of God because the first thing about prayer is protection from all the tricks that the devil may try to pull on you. Remember that, as believers in Christ, we are the number one enemies of the devil, and he will go extra miles just to deceive us out of the promises God has for you.

The second book of this series, which coming is 'The ultimate weapon is Prayer," and the third one will be The promises of God IN HIM are 'Yes and IN HIM Amen...."

Now, before getting into the text , I want you first to understand that we put on our armor, and then we know the power of prayer so that we can receive the manifestation of the promises of God. We need to understand that we are in a war.

This is spiritual warfare, and how do we Engage the Enemy?

The Weapons of our warfare is Mighty. We don't need human's plans or methods to win our battles. Satan's stronghold is the world's way to fight. But, we prefer, and thus, will follow God's way.

> 2 Corinthians 10:4 For the weapons of our warfare are not [a]carnal but mighty in God for pulling down strongholds.

God's weapons are {Prayer, fasting, faith, hope, love}, Gods word Praise, testimony, the holy spirit and the gifts of the Holy Spirit are potent and effective (Eph 6:13-18)

Two Invisible Spiritual Kingdoms (The kingdom of God & the kingdom of Satan)

We should know that ours is not a natural battle but spiritual warfare and that there are two invisible spiritual kingdoms - the kingdom of God and the kingdom of Satan. The people who work for the Kingdom of God operate in the spirit realms in faith. This is what keeps them going, and what also keeps them showing more signs of confidence that they will win all their life battles.

But, those who operate in the kingdom of Satan are driven by fear, and also use fear to control the minds of others. Whenever they want believers to do something which is not in line with the word of God, they make sure to first plant fear in their heart by warning them that something terribly wrong was about to happen. So, if you are not actively reading the word of God, we will miss that part which says we defeated the devil by the word of our testimony [Revelations 12 verse 11]. Always cast out the fear which the devil try's to plant in our mind.

Being a believer means more than belonging to God but being his servant, his disciple. Being God's disciple, you are subjected to many battles in which we must use the word of the Lord against the devil and win.

Military terminology warfare against sin & Satan

Like I have already mentioned, we are in a spiritual battle, and it will be helpful for us to treat this like it's a real military confrontation. In this battle, God must be commander in chief. Our thoughts must be submitted to his control, capture every though to yield to Christ.

casting down arguments and every high thing that exalts itself against the knowledge of God, bringing

every thought into captivity to the obedience of Christ,
2 Corinthians 10:5

When exposed to ideas or wrong opportunities, you have a choice. Pride is what keeps people from a relationship with Christ.

God is conceren about every thing that concerns you. He cares about us. He loves us. Yet our pride often blinds us to his love. When we are proud, we forget that God has personal feelings about us, and we lose our own beliefs about God.

Understanding Pride

[1] Jesus left that part of the country and returned with his disciples to Nazareth, his hometown. [2] The next Sabbath, he began teaching in the synagogue, and many who heard him were amazed. They asked, "Where did he get all this wisdom and the power to perform such miracles?" [3] Then they scoffed, "He's just a carpenter, the son of Mary and the brother of James, Joseph, Judas, and Simon. And his sisters live right here among us." *They were deeply offended and refused to believe in him.* [4] Then Jesus told them, "A prophet is honored everywhere except in his own hometown, and among his relatives and his own family." [5] And because of their unbelief, he couldn't do any miracles

among them except to place his hands on a few sick people and heal them. [6] And he was amazed at their unbelief. Then Jesus went from village to village, teaching the people.

–Mark 6:1-6 (NLT)

Speaking of pride, I want to remind you of the spiritual Kingdoms that exist. These TWO INVISIBLE SPIRITUAL KINGDOMS are the kingdom of God and Satan. The kingdom of God is automatically at war with the kingdom of Satan. You chose your side when you got saved YOU ARE ON THE LORDS SIDE – the kingdom of God – which also automatically sets you up on a clash against Satan.

"Helmet of Salvation."

The helmet protects the head—perhaps the most vital part of the body since it is the seat of thought and the mind. When we have a sure knowledge of our salvation, we will not be moved by Satan's deceptions. When we are certain that we are in Christ with our sins forgiven, we will have a peace that nothing can disturb.

We want to be dressed for the battle and we need the **"Helmet of Salvation."** A helmet is vital for survival in warfare for protecting the brain, the command station for the rest of the body. If the head is damaged, the rest of the armor would be of little use. Apostle Paul used the armor of the Roman soldier as a metaphor of our spiritual attire because this is how we, as Christians, get victory over Satan.

The spiritual Battle Takes Place in Our Mind

We understand that we are in a spiritual battle, and this battle takes place in our minds. When there is spiritual warfare, the Bible teaches us that we wrestle not against flesh and blood (Ephesians 6:12) but we wrestle in our minds. Satan wants to control your mind; he is not fighting you physically.

When someone is against you, attacking you physically or in other kinds of ways, the likeliest thing is they are being oppressed by demonic activities taking place in their mind. But, when you put on the "Helmet of Salvation" you receive Jesus Christ as your Lord and Savior. And your mind begins to "change" such that demons cannot oppress it anymore. The Bible calls that "change" the renewal of your mind (Romans 12:2).

When your mind is being renewed, you don't think the way you used to, but you think the way the Bible teaches you to think because all this time, your mind is being cleansed by the word of God.

In the movie Concussion, which stars Will Smith. The film spoke about how, when two players get a head-to-head collision while playing football can have a "concussion." And, when they get the "concussion," the rest of their body functions will not operate properly because their brain would have been injured.

Likewise, if our mind is not thinking right, we cannot operate properly, because it would have been injured. Therefore, as Christians, we must be mindful of the things that we think and allow into our minds.

The brain is to the body as the mind is to the soul. It is the control center. The brain is the control center for the mind, and the mind is the control center for the soul. Your brain tells you what to do, making it the control center for the functions of the body. Likewise, the mind is the control center for the soul. What is in your soul? What does it look like? Your mind, your will, your emotion, and your intellect are all in your soul.

The intention was that God would lead us by our spirit; but then the fall came, and separation from God. Man began to live according to the lusts

The desires that we experience that go against God's will. In other words, a desire for anything sinful. See James 1:14. Also called "sin in the flesh." Although the expression "youthful lusts" is often thought of in... in his body. (Genesis 3:6)

Because the body took over the leadership, we are earthly by nature – carnal and not spiritual. Our lives are in the things that have been created, and we naturally worship the greatness of this world. Our soul – our senses – revolve around the visible things. The truth is that we are restless in this state, and we suffer under the emptiness of this world, for our spirit can never be content or satisfied by the things that have been created.

It is possible, through the word of God , to be converted to God. Instead of loving our lusts, we can act according to Jesus' words: "Take up your cross daily and deny yourself." (Luke 9:23) By denying ourselves, our spirit is delivered from the sin in our flesh, and we enter into fellowship with God. And then, as we start to nourish ourselves with God's Word and prayer, we receive strength to discipline our body and bring it into subjection. (1 Corinthians 9:27)

There is a spirit man inside of you, and once you accept Jesus Christ as your Lord and savior, the spirit man awakes. When you accept Jesus Christ as your Lord and Savior, you begin to live life on the Lord's side. And, if you are on the Lord's side, believe it or not, Satan is coming against you. Because he is coming for you, once you are saved, you must dress for battle and be able to stand against the fiery darts of the enemy. Failure to do so might condemn you into becoming a casualty of war.

In spiritual battles, what you think determines your victory.

.......as he thinks in his heart, so is he: (Proverbs 23:7).

Whatever you think you are, that is what you exactly are. What you think you are, you already are. If you Think you are a loser, you are a loser for real, and if you think you are a failure, you are a failure indeed. The list goes on. People who have faced various episodes of defeat in their lives first built it in their hearts; I don't wish for the same with you. Instead meditate about winning and produce these kinds of fruits on the outside.

Now let us proceed to the **Breastplate of Righteousness.**

CHAPTER TWO

THE BREASTPLATE
OF RIGHTEOUSNESS

To MOVE AHEAD FROM the previous chapter, we base this one on the book of Ephesians 6: 14. This second part, taken from my message on the Whole Armor of God, speaks about the "Breastplate of Righteousness." In this part, I will review the Breastplate of Righteousness, and you must pay attention to it because I am going to talk about the four entities that every beliver wars against.

..........For we do not wrestle against flesh and blood, but against (1) principalities, against (2) powers, against the (3) rulers of the darkness of this age, against (4) spiritual hosts of wickedness in the heavenly places (Ephesians 6:12)

Having outlined the four dimensions with which we fight against , I want to now explain a little bit on each of them in the paragraphs below.

Principalities

What are principalities? These are ranked demons, so high up in their kingdom that they have abilities beyond any human capability.

> Luke 10:19 Behold, I give you the authority to trample on serpents and scorpions, and over all the power of the enemy, and nothing shall by any means hurt you.

We are, therefore, not fighting against flesh and blood but against such powerful forces which can only be defeated by another higher force - God. These principalities are demons that create an atmosphere over a region; it could be a household, a business, your home, your marriage, or your body. This demonic atmosphere could be in the form of depression, strife, low self-esteem, excessive drive, and lack of self-control.

The devil hates your progress hence his sending of all such principalities, creating an 'overarching' atmosphere in your immediate environment just to make sure you stay down. However, we have been forewarned through the reading of the word of God. We have been encouraged to stay vigilant and, above all, trust in God so that we sour above the influence of these principalities.

Powers

The second of these entities is Powers. These are "rulers and authorities." These powers represent "the ability to control and influence." When we say power, we understand that the Holy Spirit has power because He can influence what goes on inside of you. Even if you may choose not to listen, the Holy Spirit always speaking to you, using your 'inner man' because He has the ability to do so. The Holy Spirit dwells inside of you – He is the person with the power. Now, My other book provides an in-depth teaching about the Holy Spirit. { *The Person with Power: Holy Spirit Dwelling on the Inside* } But this is not our focus; don't get this mixed up because Satan has powers too. Examples of Satan's powers are fortune-telling, Ouija boards, tarot cards, palmistry, psychic, mystic, occult, or magical activities. Understand what the devices of the devil are; when you see somebody do something supernaturally, it is not necessarily of God. Recall that the two invisible kingdoms are supernatural. And supernatural could be of God or Satan. A brilliant biblical illustration is Moses and Pharaoh's magicians (Exodus 7-11).

Rulers of the darkness of this age

The third entities are Rulers of the darkness of this age; these are responsible for secrets and deception (lies, tricks, and ignorance). These, we see in our daily lives, at work, church, home, school, and so forth. With these, it would help you more to stay vigilant, be watchful, and not fall in the same trap as everyone else. It starts as something small and meaningless.

You may easily find yourself lying about small things to the pastor or your parents. Once you go on and on until you feel nothing in your heart, then know that you might be falling into the trap of the rulers of the darkness of this age.

Spiritual hosts of wickedness in the heavenly places

The fourth and final group are spiritual hosts of wickedness in the heavenly places. These are territorial powers. They hindered the answers to Daniel's prayer for 21 days (Daniel 10:12-12). These powers control the heavenly places. Apostle Paul wrote about the third heaven, which means there is the second and first heaven. And remember, Satan is not in hell because he was kicked out of heaven to the earth. (Revelation 12:7-9).

So, these are the four entities every beliver wars against. They don't care that they have been defeated in the first place, but they keep on coming; they wait by the bushes to see if you make a single mis step. When this happens, they will be ready to try to come against you again. They will be prepared to drive you in the wrong direction. Take, for instance, if you used to use drugs, there they are readily available for you. If you use to sleep around, here come your type, if you use to steal here is the opportunity to do it all over again ….. When it happens, demonic forces want to take you down that path. You will be surprised how long it won't take to get hooked up to new friends who use, the bad girl / guy and opportunities to take what is not yours.

As a matter of fact, keep on watching, of course, God who does not sleep nor slumber (Psalm 121:4) will make sure to help you conquer all these forces. You just have to allow Him that space.

The Breastplate of Righteousness – Put It On

Believing in God is a matter of action – do what the Bible tells you to – practice what you learn and so much more! Now, we cannot only speak about the breastplate of righteousness without you putting it on, eventually.

Putting on the breastplate of righteousness protects your heart from the lies and deceits of Satan. The breastplate of righteousness refers to the righteousness purchased for us by Jesus Christ at the cross. We are righteous because God said we are. Moreover, we are righteous because it is a gift God gave us (Romans 5:17).

You can receive a gift and choose not to open it. If you decide not to open it, it makes no difference whether you received the gift or not.

Likewise, when Apostle Paul said to put on the whole armor of God, it meant you have the option of not putting it on. You can put on the breastplate of righteousness or not; the choice is yours. But, when you put on the breastplate of righteousness, then you are dressed with one of the six pieces of the armor for war. In this battle, we have to understand that Satan is already defeated. (Revelation 12:7-9) So, you come into spiritual warfare from a place of victory. You don't come from a place of defeat because you are already victorious (Romans 8:37). This should give you enough courage to put on the armor and march into the battlefield with your head healed high.

The bible says greater is he who is in you than he who is in the world (1 John 4:4 and 1 John 5:4), meaning that you are saved already and won the battle against Satan. You are on the winning team – the kingdom of God (Colossians 1:13). You won, and you always win. In the sports circles, they call this a delayed match where the results are already known even before you get to watch the game on TV.

Believing in these teachings means that you are rightly acting as the one who stands for the Lord here on earth. Now that you are saved you are ambassadors, a representative of Jesus Christ on earth, let's go to 2nd Corinthians to see who an ambassador is.

> .... Now then, we are ambassadors for Christ, as though God were pleading through us: we implore you on Christ's behalf, be reconciled to God. For He made Him who knew no sin to be sin for us, that we might become the righteousness of God in Him.
>
> (2nd Corinthians 5:20-21)

How do we become the righteousness of God? From these scriptures, we become the righteousness of God in Jesus Christ. We also understand, though citizens of heaven, we are ambassadors of Jesus Christ here on earth, which means that we have the ability to demonstrate all the powers that Jesus Christ had and even more as He has said in the word of God.

> ....Verily, verily, I say unto you, He that believeth on me, the works that I do shall he also do; and greater works than these shall he do; because I go unto my Father (John 14:12).

Again you have a choice to operate in this power or not. Nonetheless, it is available to you. Knowing that we are Jesus Christ's ambassadors means we can do the works he did because we have the Holy Spirit living on the inside of us. Take an example of a US ambassador in any country; that person has the power to act on behalf of the country. If by any means, people in that country decide to kill the US ambassador, it will be counted as an act of war against the US. As such, you are representing God while here on earth, know that and let it give you courage that God has you.

> With the power of the Holy Spirit, I can do all things through Christ who strengthens me. (Philippians 4:13).

Missing the Mark

When you received Jesus Christ, God automatically gave you an A grade. We all got an A. but how do we drop from an A to a B+? Because we missed the mark, missing the mark is another term for **SIN**.

Every time we missed the mark, we go from an A to a B+. The more we missed the mark, the further we dropped from grade A, which means drifting away from God. We can miss the mark and drift so far we can't seem to feel God's presence anymore. Then, we complain we can't feel God's presence and say He has moved or shifted places?. God hasn't moved, you moved. When you had an A, you were right there in fellowship with Him and Jesus Christ.

But, the moment you drifted, you scored a lower grade and lost the fellowship, then you missed the mark and drifted further. When you drift away from God, that is the time you begin hearing all these strange voices, being put under the influences of the principalities we once spoke about. Now you hear Satan's voice and can't hear God clearly. Like Eve in the garden, you listen to Satan's lies. Eve got into a conversation with the serpent, and he lied to her. It wasn't a bald-faced lie because Eve would have become suspicious. He deceived using half-truth. A half-truth is a whole lie. If you have drifted from God believing Satan's half-truths, reconcile with God now, enjoy His fellowship and feel His awesome presence !!

Your righteous acts are no match for Satan's attacks. So, when, you received Jesus Christ, he instantly gave you a breastplate. The breastplate is designed by God to protect your heart. Satan operates in evil and deception. He always wants to deceive you. He is a liar. And everything he comes to tell you is a lie. Remember the bible says he is the father of lies. (John 8:44 and 2 Corinthians 11:3)

In Isaiah 64:4-8, Isaiah the prophet spoke about righteousness and God's anger when his people missed the mark. Likewise, though we missed the mark and God got angry, He gave us opportunities for repentance through Jesus Christ, the only one who can cleanse us and bring us back into the presence of God. It does not matter how far you went from God, the truth is you always have the gift of righteousness, the question is, are you going to open the gift? When we repent of our sins, God is always waiting to welcome us back. We often think God has left us, but the truth is He never left, rather we left him.

So, when we repent He is always happy. Will you repent now?

There are three steps to repentance.

I. The first step is to confess your sin
II. The second step is turning away from the sin, and the
III. The third step is to turn to the obedience of the word of God

Once you repent from your sin, you cannot go back there again, because it is like going back to your vomit (Proverbs 26:11 and 2 Peter 2:20-22). You know those things you need to turn away from. Whatever your schemes are or whatever is tripping you up, those are the sins you have to turn away from.

The Breastplate of FAITH and LOVE

But let us who are of the day be sober, putting on the breastplate of faith and love, and as a helmet the hope of salvation (1 Thessalonians 5:8)

When we talk about the Breastplate of Righteousness, we need to understand from the scriptures that the foundation for the Breastplate of Righteousness is Faith and Love. How do we come to know Christ? We come to know Him through Faith. It was not our works that earned us salvation but our Faith. Similarly, with the gifts of Jesus Christ, none of them did we receive by our works, but received them through Faith in Jesus Christ.

Understand that if you don't have FAITH and you don't have LOVE it is impossible to have on the Breastplate of Righteousness.

> And be found in Him, not having my own righteousness, which is from the law, but that which is through faith in Christ, the righteousness which is from God by faith (Philippians 3:9)

CHAPTER THREE

THE BELT OF TRUTH

"Stand therefore, having girded your waist with truth," Paul says. Truth is the belt that holds all the other pieces of the armor in place. There are two ways in which truth is a part of the armor of God.

First, it refers to the truths of Scripture as opposed to the lies of Satan. Satan is the father of lies (John 8:44). Jesus said, "You shall know the truth, and the truth shall make you free" (verse 32). The great truths of the Bible—the love of God, salvation through faith in Jesus Christ, the Second Coming, forgiveness of sin, grace and power to live for Jesus—these truths set us free from Satan's lies.

The second way that truth serves as a belt, holding together the full armor of God, is our personal commitment to truth—to living a life that is upright, transparent, and without deceit.

. . . .

To put on the Breastplate of Righteousness, we must first have the Belt of Truth firmly in place. Without truth, our righteousness will be based on our own attempts to impress God. This leads to legalism or self-condemnation (Romans 8:1).

We choose, instead, to acknowledge that, without Christ, we can do nothing (John 15:5). We see ourselves "in Christ" and that, regardless of our failures and achievements, His Righteousness by His Grace has been credited to our account. If Jesus is not part of what we do, the scriptures say our righteousness is like filthy rags (Isaiah 64:6 and Romans 3:19-23). There is nothing we can do to earn the righteousness of God. The righteousness of God is a gift. The only reason we are righteous is that God accords us His righteousness. (Romans 5:17 and Ephesians 2:8-9).

Without the Truth, we are lost, and the schemes of the devil will surely overpower us. Girding your waist with the Belt of Truth means holding on to the Truth and things you know are true. Understand the Bible said gird your waist with the Belt of Truth. That means you can choose to put on the Belt of Truth or not. If you choose to put on the Belt of Truth, the Truth will protect you from the lies of Satan. The word of God is Truth. Nothing compares with the word of God. If you want to know the Truth, get in the word of God. Jesus Christ is the Truth. The scriptures say Jesus Christ is "the Way, the Truth, and the Life" and it is only through Him that we come to God. (John 14:6).

Jesus Christ is the Truth, and nobody was born like Him, nobody lived like Him. Nobody prays like Jesus Christ, nobody preaches like Him, nobody teaches like Him, and nobody talks like Him. Nobody died like He did, and nobody rose again like Jesus Christ. Most definitely, nobody is coming back like Jesus Christ. Nobody is like Jesus Christ. And nobody will do you like Jesus Christ.

The hymn writer Andraé Edward Crouch (July 1, 1942 – January 8, 2015) wrote;

Can't nobody do me like Jesus.
Can't nobody do me like the Lord.
Can't nobody do me like Jesus.
He's my friend.…
He healed my body (Then He told me to run on)
I said He healed my body (Then He told me to run on)
Don't you know He healed my body (Then He told me to run on?)
He's my friend

Truth is of utmost importance in the life of a Christian. Without the Belt of Truth, the rest of the armor would be of little use to us because we would not have the Spirit of Truth.

According to the scriptures;

The word of God is TRUTH (John 17:17)

Jesus Christ is the TRUTH (John 14:6)

We worship God in Spirit and TRUTH. (John 4:24)

The Holy Spirit is called the Spirit of TRUTH (John 16:13)

God is the God of TRUTH (Deuteronomy 32:4; Isaiah 65:16)

The Gospel is called the word of TRUTH (2 Timothy 2:15)

The gospel is called the message of TRUTH (Ephesians 1:13-14)

Living a Godly life is called walking in the TRUTH (3 John 3-4)

The church is called the pillar and foundation of TRUTH (1Timothy 3:15)

Everything in the Christian Faith Is Based On the **TRUTH**. Not this modern-day relative truth, but the Absolute Truth of God.

I want you to understand that the Belt of Truth is the foundation of everything that we do as Christians.

And you shall know the truth, and the truth shall make you free. (John 8:32).

But when the Helper comes, whom I shall send to you from the Father, the Spirit of truth who proceeds from the Father, He will testify of Me. And you also will bear witness, because you have been with Me from the beginning. (John 15:26-27).

The word of God said when you know the truth; the truth will make you free, on the contrary, the world says the truth hurts. As a result, some don't want to embrace the truth because the truth will hurt them. But, according to scriptures, the truth will make you free.

How does the truth make you free?

As you come to know the truth, the truth helps you realize and recognize your ills. The truth also helps you to realize and recognize what God has truly done for you. So, you have to walk in the truth of God. As Christians, we must operate in truth, operating in truth means we are open, and we are honest, even if it is going to hurt somebody's feelings. It means we need to tell the truth at all costs. When I say at all cost I mean at all costs and not some cost.

Did you know? You can live to testify of the truth even if you do not say a word about it. Equally, you can live to testify of the false things which the devil brings to the world.

We need to know those things which give Satan praises to avoid them.

Also, don't get caught up in religious clichés that glorify Satan. Number one of such lies of Satan is; "THE DEVIL IS BUSY." You are praising and worshipping Satan when you say the devil is busy, you are giving him his worth. And most of the time we give him credit for our wrong choices. Another brilliant example of Christian cliché is "God never gives us more than we can handle." How about those who commit suicide? Do you think they wanted to be there? People commit suicide when Satan gets hold of their mind and controls it, remember our conversation at the beginning of this book.

We have no business giving the devil praises because our God is greater and Satan is defeated already. Jesus Christ has the victory.

The Mind - the Battle Ground for Spiritual Warfare

Spiritual battles are fought in the Mind. To break down Satan's deception you have to bring your mind into submission and obedience to the truth of God's Word. Understand the strongholds of the enemy are prejudice, unbelief, and mental blockage to the things which God wants us to have. You have to see your victory, for the Scriptures say, on the Cross, Jesus Christ totally defeated Satan!!!

It is our responsibility to demonstrate the victory that Jesus Christ already won for us. It is also our responsibility to make proper use of the weapons which God has equipped us with. Putting on the **"Belt of Truth"** is a lifestyle of honesty, sincerity, openness, and frankness. Having, said that, these teachings continue with demonic attacks against your mind through spiritual warfare known as witchcraft.

Demonic Attacks against Your Mind through Spiritual Warfare Known as Witchcraft

Satan operates in lies and deceptions. The power he uses to deceive and manipulate people is lies, tricks, and half-truths. He uses these gimmicks to get you to believe his lies. Just like when he met Eve in the garden, (Genesis 3) he manipulated her by asking the question Eve already knew just to create doubt in her. "Did God say you shall not eat of every tree of the garden?" This question was deceptive because God never said they should not eat of every tree in the garden.

Satan manipulated Eve to disobey God by eating from the tree of knowledge of good and evil. Eve gave to Adam and he ate. Instantly they became aware of the nakedness and lost their fellowship with God. They sew figs trees to cover their nakedness, and they were half-naked.

As a result, when God visited, they were hiding. God asked where they were. God asked them what they knew. Likewise, God is asking you where you are on your Christian journey. Do you know where you are on your Christian journey? Are you crystal clear on whose side you are? Do you know who your Satan is?

Your, Satan is your sin.

Society has painted what Satan is like, but can I tell you Satan isn't any of those pictures you see on comic books or movies, but, your Satan is the one you have.

Different people have different manifestations of Satan; whatever makes you disobey God is your Satan. Or, whatever makes you do the things which are going the opposite direction to what God says is your own version of Satan. Whatsoever Satan you have is the one that will tempt you into disobeying God.

We do know that with every temptation, God has set aside an alternative for escape. So, for every temptation, there is a way of escape. The way out of temptation is sitting right beside the temptation. Are you going to accept Satan's lies and fall into temptation? Or, do the right thing and take the way of escape. The Bible in (1 Thessalonians 5:22) said, abstain from all appearances of evil, to abstain means to refrain, or withdraw, it means to escape. You don't have the luxury of engaging

Satan in a conversation like Eve did; because the word said to abstain from all appearances of evil.

When it smells Satan before you get burnt beloved, use the fire exit. The devil is cunning, he will find a way to sneak into your life and before you know it, you would have long strayed from the path of God.

The Devil Never Shows Up in A Red Suit With A Pitchfork And Horns Displaying His Evil. No!!

Like we have said, the devil understands the language of deception very well. So, he is never going to obviously reveal himself to you, not at all! Satan dresses like an angel of light to deceive. And no marvel; for Satan himself is transformed into an angel of light. (2 Corinthians 11:14).

When Satan comes to you he is not going to look like temptation. Often, he looks like an angel of light. But, when you are caught in his ploy that is when the mess shows up. I was thinking the other day how movies glorify sex before marriage. They show all the interesting and pleasurable part, but, they don't show the mess and heartbreaks that come with it. They neither show young girls getting pregnant nor do they show the single mothers trying to raise her young baby alone. They don't show the young single mothers going back to school and raising her child all by herself. They don't show the guy responsible for her pregnancy walking away leaving the young girl all by herself raising the child. They don't show drug addicts, alcoholics, people fighting depression, and having Gender identity crises. This brings us to the four components of witchcraft attacks; Domination and Control, Manipulation, Deception, and Intimidation.

1. **Domination and Control** - They come as one package. Somebody is controlling or trying to dominate you.

2. **Manipulation** - that is when somebody tries to manipulate or trick you to do something they want you to do. The use of a trick is for you to eventually find yourself knee-deep into something you would rather have not gotten involved with.

3. **Deception** - If you are proceeding in some way, mostly the unlawful short cut, and you know that there is another way, that itself is deception (Proverbs 26:12). It comes under the umprella of witchcraft.

4. **Intimidation** – To intimidate somebody into doing something is religious witchcraft—which often manifests as intimidation, manipulation and maligning—don't try to defend yourself. Let the Lord vindicate you. Don't stop doing what God told you to do. Keep pressing into your Kingdom assignment with confidence that He has your back.

Usually, that 'something' they are supposed to do will not be in line with the word of God.

In Luke 9:1, Jesus gave His disciples authority over 'all demons.' For every beliver who realises they have been attacked by the spirit of fear and intimidation or any other spiritual reality, they must first recognise that Christ has given them authority over all the works of the enemy and second they must apply this victory to their life.

Normally, women flow in the manipulation part and men flow in the intimidation part, but it can go either way.

Finally, witchcraft works against the flesh (Galatians 5:19). In our fallen nature, there are two aspects of witchcraft, the natural and supernatural. The natural is the flesh and the supernatural are demonic activities. I will talk about the supernatural aspect of witchcraft, which is demonic activities. And under this subject, I shall talk about common demonic attacks against your mind through witchcraft.

Common Demonic Attacks against your mind through Witchcraft.

1. **Confusion** – One of the obvious routes of witchcraft attacks against you is confusion. You are confused and can't seem to decide; you can't grasp what is

going on in your mind. You keep losing things, your keys, your phone, and your wallet.

2. **Isolation** – This means avoiding people. You don't want to talk to people at all. If you don't want to be around people, know that the spirit of depression is coming on you. Depression is a device of the enemy. I was depressed for almost two years, yet I didn't know I was. How did I eventually know I was depressed? I went to a Bible study one night and the lady teaching spoke about how depression feels like. She said the following;

   I. She said when you are depressed you just don't feel like yourself, and I said, yes, I don't feel like myself.

   II. She said you don't want to go anywhere, and said yeah, that is true, I don't want to go anywhere.

   III. Finally, she said you normally want to be around people but now you don't want to be around people. And I confirmed, I don't want to be around people.

I said oh my, I am depressed. From that point on, she spoke about how you can be removed or delivered from depression. And she went on to talk about the sword of the spirit, which is the word of God. (Ephesians 6:17). The word of God is what you require to be delivered from depression. You need to get saturated in the word. Like when you are hungry, your stomach is roaring for food, also, if you are depressed your spirit is thirsty for the word of God.

Once you start feeding your spirit with the word of God, you will gradually come out of that depression. But first, you have to recognize what is going on because you can't conquer what you won't confess to.

Some Biblical Weapons to Fight Depression

- Lean not on your own understanding (Proverbs 3:5-6)
- The word of God - the sword of the spirit (Ephesians 6:17)
- Also, you have to plead the blood of Jesus (Revelation 12:11)
- Understand that God has not given you the spirit of fear but that of sound mind (2 Timothy 1:7)
- You acknowledge that greater is he who is in you than he who is in the world (1 John 4:4)

3. **Fear** - Fear is under the umbrella of witchcraft. When you are under the spirit of fear, you don't seem to make any decision. If you can't decide, you are under the attack of witchcraft. If you are walking around with fear, it means you are paralyzed by fear. And, when you are paralyzed by fear, you can't

decide. Confess the word of God in (2 Timothy) to conquer the spirit of fear and depression.

For God has not given us a spirit of fear, but of power and of love and a sound mind. Sometimes you have to recite (2 Timothy 1:7).

You can't conquer what you won't confess to, thus, confess whatever is binding you first and expect to get the victory over it. No matter what, if you won't confess, you won't have victory over it. I don't mean going about telling everything that has ever happened to you. But, you need to be confident enough to confess your burdens. When you confess, you empower yourself to victory. Whatever it was that was bothering you, it won't bind you anymore.

4. **You magnify your faults** - When you are under the attack of witchcraft, you magnify your wrongs and faults, your thoughts are negative, and you become critical of others. It may, however, happen to you, but as you dwell on those negative thoughts, make sure you do not voice them. Never vocalize whatever negative thought you are thinking of. If you do, you empower the enemy, and Satan gets hold of your mind. SPEAK LIFE !!!

As a believer , we are not meant to be in that place. I am bringing these to your attention so that you don't open up a crack, in your wall of life, for witchcraft. If you open up a crack for witchcraft then, more things can come in from the crack.

5. **You have vain imagination** - This means you imagine things in your mind, those things don't necessarily have to happen but in your mind, it already happened. Such imaginations are dangerous as they can make you have fearful , worrisome And anxious pitures in your mind.

> Because that, when they knew God, they glorified him not as God, neither were thankful; but became vain in their imaginations, and their foolish heart was darkened (Romans 1:21).

These imaginations are negative; they are evil because they don't edify God nor do they glorify the body of Christ - the church. Romans 21 teaches, because we do not want to glorify God, we imagine vain things and that is the device of the enemy, getting in those thoughts allows the enemy to strike. But the Bible showed us what things we should fill our minds with.

Finally, brethren, whatsoever things are true, whatsoever things are honest, whatsoever things are just, whatsoever things are pure, whatsoever things are lovely, whatsoever things are of good report; if there be any virtue, and if there be any praise, think on these things. (Philippians 4:8).

Summary
Casting down Arguments

Casting down arguments and every high thing that exalts itself against the knowledge of God, bringing every thought into captivity to the obedience of Christ (2 Corinthians 10:5)

The work of Jesus Christ on the cross defeated Satan and all of his demons. You need to know what you believe in, and why you do so. I am not talking about knowledge, I am talking about conviction. There is a difference between the ones who blindly follow some teachings and the ones who are convicted of what he or she believes in.

There is something important you should understand here. You hold beliefs (knowledge), but, convictions hold you. When you have convictions, they, indeed, hold you. They shape your thinking, your attitude, and responses to life issues and situations. Whenever you want to respond to any situation, your first point of call is to ask what God thinks about it because you have the conviction that He is the one who is working all things together for my good. Understand that the Christian Faith is more of conviction and less of comfort.

> For I am convinced that neither death nor life, neither angels nor demons, neither the present nor the future, nor any powers, neither height nor depth, nor anything else in all creation, will be able to separate us from the love of God that is in Christ Jesus our Lord. (Romans 8:38-39)

Nothing can separate you from the love of God. God loves you above everything else. If you did not believe that, you can now believe this truth because He gave us his only son – to let him die on the cross for our sins. Recognize that this is the place of conviction you must come from. No matter what you have been through, or what you have done, or where you have been. God loves you. Leave your past behind and move ahead. Apostle Paul said;

> Not that I have already attained, or am already perfected; but I press on, that I may lay hold of that for

which Christ Jesus has also laid hold of me. Brethren, I do not count myself to have apprehended; but one thing I do, forgetting those things which are behind and reaching forward to those things which are ahead, I press toward the goal for the prize of the upward call of God in Christ Jesus (Philippians 3:12-14).

Therefore, if anyone is in Christ, he is a new creation; old things have passed away; behold, all things have become new. (2nd Corinthians 5:17).

As a way to push in a little further, I want to make it crystal clear that there are two invisible spiritual kingdoms (the kingdom of God and the kingdom of Satan). These two kingdoms are at war against each other all the time.

Finally, brethren, when you allow thoughts of fear, defeat, and failure, the same as allowing witchcraft to get into your mind. Therefore, when Satan comes against you through witchcraft, engage him with the word of God. When he tempted Jesus Christ, the Lord defeated him with the word of God. Jesus Christ said, "it is written…." (Matthew 4:4-6)

Likewise, when Satan comes against you, tell him it is written!

CHAPTER FOUR

THE SHIELD
OF FAITH

I HAVE BEEN TALKING ABOUT putting on the whole
Armor of God with the understanding that you are
in spiritual warfare. And, because you are saved, by
default you are on the Lord's side, that is, if you profess
Jesus Christ as your Lord and Savior, you are on the
His side. Being on the Lord's side means the enemy is
going to attack you every chance he gets because you
are saved.

In this chapter, our emphasis is on (Ephesians 6:16)

**Above all, taking the shield of faith with which you will
be able to quench all the fiery darts of the wicked one.**

Your shield of faith in spiritual battle is your protection.
The Shield of faith protects you against the fiery darts of

the enemy. Understand that, from the previous chapters, our warfare is not with flesh and blood, but against principalities, powers, the rulers of the darkness of this age, and spiritual hosts of wickedness in the heavenly places. (Ephesians 6:12)

So, if you have an issue with somebody or somebody is not treating you right, you need to know that it is not a physical battle and your issue is not with that person but with the spirit behind the person. You must recognize when the devil cunningly disguises himself as your brother or sister just to attack you. You must not fall into his plans like Eve and Adam.

Paul was in prison under the guard of Roman soldiers when he wrote the book of Ephesians. He observed the natural appearances of the Roman soldiers and how they were dressed. He flipped it around and compared it to the spiritual dress of the believers. Because the Roman soldiers were in a natural war, they were dressed naturally, likewise, because we are in supernatural warfare, we are dressed supernaturally.

When we are in warfare, the battle is in our minds, and there are two invisible spiritual kingdoms, the kingdom of God and the kingdom of Satan. The kingdom God is contending for your mind, same as Satan is contending for the same mind, which is the reason why our spiritual battles take place in our mind. Satan is the world's way of doing things which is contrary to God's way of doing things. When our mind is renewed (Romans 12:2), that is when we start doing things God's way! If we don't take out time to renew our minds, there is no way we are going to do things the way God instructs us to. This leads us to the subject of Faith in(not necessary) (Hebrew 11:6).

> **But, without faith, it is impossible to please Him, for he who comes to God must believe that He is and that He is a rewarder of those who diligently seek Him. (Hebrew 11:6)**

When you don't have faith, it is impossible to please God. This could be interpreted as, if, you don't have faith you are not saved, because the scriptures say that by grace you are saved through faith. (Ephesians 2:8) Every time that you professed Jesus Christ as your Lord and Savior, you took a step of faith. In (Hebrew 11:6), you understand that he who comes to God must believe not only that He is God, but that He is the Trinity. He is God: The Father, God: The Son, and God: The Holy Spirit living in the inside of you.

So you have to;
Believe that He is the Healer (Exodus15:26)
Believe that He is the Savior (Titus 2:13)

Believe that He is the Deliverer (Psalm 116)

Believe that He is the Redeemer (Isaiah 47:4)

Believe that He is the Great I Am (Exodus 3:14)

Believe that He is the Provider (Genesis 22:14)

Believe that He is the Supplier (Philippians 4:19)

Believe that He the Promise Keeper (Luke 1:1-25)

Believe that He is the Supreme Being (Isaiah 44:6)

Believe that He is the author and finisher of our faith (Hebrews 12:2)

Believe that He is a rewarder of those that diligently seek him (Hebrews 11:6)

The shield of faith is necessary to withstand the attacks of the devil, and (Ephesians 6:16) says,

> **In addition to all this, take up the shield of faith, with which you can extinguish all the flaming arrows of the evil one. (NIV)**

The Roman shield is not small and you can't hold in your hand if you are not trained on how to hold and use it. It is 4 feet (1.22 meters), high and 2 feet (0.61 meters) wide.

The Shield of Faith – Ephesians 6:16

The shield can cover the soldiers or the believer's whole body. It is high and wide enough to protect your whole body so you can defend yourself against the flaming dart of the enemy. Knowing that;

> Whatever is born of God overcomes the world. And this is the victory that has overcome the world even our faith. (1st John 5:4),

This scripture confirms that your faith is the victory that overcomes the world. Therefore;

Faith is seeing the invisible,
Touching the intangible,
Believing the impossible
Moving forward as it is possible.

Subsequently, this understanding is going to be our working definition of faith. When you have faith, you need to know that it doesn't matter what situations you are in, you already have the victory because faith is a supernatural and universal phenomenon. Faith is the supernatural currency that, when used here on earth, moves the hand of God.

Faith Is SUBSTANTIAL and Faith Is the EVIDENCE

> Now faith is the substance of things hoped for, the evidence of things not seen. (Hebrews 11:1)

In heavenly transactions, we must understand that Faith is the currency of exchange (Hebrews 11:6). Faith is the substance in the realm of the spirit, in other words, it is the plug that connects you to the fuse of the heavenly, and allows you to withdraw from the Heavens' account. If your faith is not connecting you to heaven, it means your faith is not operating properly. You know, when your lamp is not properly plugged in when you pushed the switch to on and the light doesn't turn on until the lamp is properly plugged in to connect with the source of power. Likewise, your faith needs to be connected to heaven to operate properly.

How do we get plugged into heaven's power? Through our prayers, praises, worship, and the time we spend in His presence. On a final note, know that Faith is the evidence that keeps you connected to God.

Having said that, I believe in my SANCTIFIED IMAGINATION that God likes evidence because I have seen, from the scriptures, the things He did so there could be evidence. You understand that in a lawsuit, you must have evidence to convict someone of a crime. Likewise, God uses evidence to demonstrate His power.

Under the law, without credible verifiable evidence, you cannot convict someone of a crime.

So, we do have the cliché that we have grown so used to:

****You Are Innocent Until Proven Guilty *****

Now that, we recognize faith is evidence; the question is how can faith be evidence if it is invisible? Reflecting on this perception, the first suggestion that came to my mind is the wind - you cannot see the wind but you know it is there, how do I know the wind is there? I know the wind is there because I have the evidence. These pieces of evidence are:

When I see the trees sway, that lets me know the wind is there

When I see the dresses blow, that lets me know the wind is there

When I see the hair flow, that lets me know the wind is there

This is some evidence that shows that the wind is there even when it is invisible.

Reiterating that God likes evidence, let me confirm this further, from the scriptures.

Jesus Christ Walks on the Water
– (Matthew 14:22-33)

Knowing that faith is invisible, one of the shreds of evidence that Jesus Christ shows us, through the scriptures, was when the disciples were at the sea and there was a storm (Matthew 14:22-33).

The disciples were at sea after Jesus Christ instructed them to get in the boat to move to the other side before him while he dismisses the crowd. A storm arose, and the boat was in the middle of the sea, tossed by the waves because the wind was contrary. The disciples were in despair. But Jesus Christ went to them, walking on the water. His walking on the waves was the evidence that the supernatural was present. He could have remained at the seashore, then ordered the boat to float to the beach, better still command the storm and wave to be still like he did in (Matthew 8:23-26).

Jesus Christ Is Raised (Matthew 28:1-2)

When Jesus rose from the dead on the first day of the week, Mary Magdalene and the other Mary, and certain another woman with them, came to the tomb bringing the spices which they had prepared. But, they found the stone rolled away from the tomb and the angel of the Lord sitting on it. Then, they went in and did not find the body of the Lord Jesus Christ. This, again happened so that they can have the evidence of his resurrection.

Couldn't Jesus Christ walk out of the tomb through the stone? Yes, he could, but, he wanted there to be the evidence that he rose.

Moses at the Red Sea
(Exodus 12:29-51; 14:15-21; 14:1-30)

When Moses was to lead the Israelites out of Egypt, he went several times to Pharaoh asking him to "Let God's people go." But, Pharaoh wouldn't listen. Eventually, after the loss of the firstborns of the Egyptians, he permitted them to go. But, afterward, he changed his mind and took his army and pursued after Moses and the Israelites.

Now Moses and the Israelites were headed towards the red sea and were sandwiched between the Egyptian Army and the red sea. Still, they pressed on towards the red sea. God the father, parted the red sea for them to pass on dry ground. Pharaoh and his army jumped on the opportunity and went through the red sea on dry ground. But when the last Israelite stepped out of the red sea, Moses closed the red sea and Pharaoh and his army. This again shows that God likes evidence.

The Woman with Issue of Blood
(Matthew 9:20–22)

The last example of God using evidence is about the woman with the issue of blood for 12 years. This woman came pressing through the crowd confessing if she can touch the helm of Jesus Christ's garment she will be made whole. She had faith in her mind and she spoke faith out of her mouth, that all she needed was a touch of his garment, so she kept pushing against the crowd until she touched him and, she was made whole instantly. This woman had faith in her mind and did exactly what she said she was going to do.

What is it that you said you are going to do? What are you saying that you are going to do? Whatever you say you are going to do in your mind; that is exactly what is going to happen.

Jesus Christ was in the midst of the crowd which thronging him. He stopped and said, 'Who touched me?' Everyone was touching Jesus Christ, but when this woman touched him, she pulled virtue out of Jesus Christ's body. When you touch Jesus Christ, you are pulling at his virtue. Observe that the Bible didn't say she was healed. But, that she was made whole. Whole means, "nothing missing and nothing broken." This woman got whole spiritually, financially, and mentally, everything about her was whole. This was the evidence that she met with Jesus Christ.

What is your evidence that you have been with Jesus Christ?

As the body without the spirit is dead, so, faith without works is dead (James 2:26)

For your faith to work, you have a part to play, there is something you have to do. You can't keep saying it and not put some actions to it because faith without action is dead. Now, the question of this hour is what is FAITH?

Faith is seeing the invisible, touching the intangible, believing the impossible, moving forward as it is possible.

Faith Is Not Encouragement but Empowerment

In Faith, we have to be fully persuaded that the word of God is TRUTH. Being fully persuaded, we will be able to work out that Faith is not encouragement but empowerment. Faith is a spiritual weapon because it is listed in (Ephesians 6:16). There are different kinds of faiths but, the Shield of Faith is a Spiritual Weapon. As you go deeper into the scriptures, you'll find out that faith for salvation is different from faith for spiritual warfare. But, understand first that God has given everyone a measure of faith (Romans 12:3)

The kinds of Faith

- Common faith - Titus 1:4
- Little faith - Matthew 8:26
- No faith - Mark 4:40
- Temporary faith - Luke 8:13
- Strong faith - Romans 4:20
- Great faith - Matthew 8:10
- Divine faith - Galatians 2:20

To dress with the shield of faith, you must know the different kinds of faith so that you can apply it correctly. If you go into a spiritual battle with faith for salvation, you are not dressed. You have to make sure that you have the right kind of faith before you go into a spiritual battle. As stated above the shield of faith protects the whole body, it protects every aspect of your life. But, what I discovered in counseling a lot of Christians is they say...

> Lord, I will give you my Sunday morning... not my Saturday Night
> Lord, I will give you my Money... not my Sex life
> Lord, I will give you my time... not my drugs and Alcohol addiction.

You know it is not only drugs and alcohol we are addicted to, but we also are addicted to food, television, sport, computer games, social media (Facebook, YouTube, Instagram, and Twitter to mention a few).

They say, Lord, I will give you my Praise... not my Worship, but the scriptures say let everything that has breathe praise the Lord (Psalms 150:6). Moreover, God said, if you don't give him praise, He will make the ROCKS cry out. (Luke 19:40).

Observe the scriptures went further to say that those that worship God must worship Him in Spirit and in truth (John 4:24) That is to say, you worship God through your spirit and through the truth of His Word. Not half-truth, but the absolute truth. Which is the word of God?

God wants your full attention because He will not share His glory with anyone (Isaiah 42:8). The definition of Faith is to rely absolutely on God. It means to trust God at His word. Knowing that our God is a jealous God (Joshua 24:19) and we need to spend quality time in His presence since He desires your praise and worship. To conclude this section, know that Faith is to rely totally upon God; that is having the confidence, connection, and conviction to trust God at His word.

Your, Shield of Faith Is Designed to Quench the Fiery Darts of the Enemy

In recapping the anchor Bible reference for this chapter;

> Above all, taking the shield of faith with which you will be able to quench all the fiery darts of the wicked one (Ephesians 6:16).

I am going to break this scripture down in case you don't understand it.

Quench, in this context, means to put out the fire. When you put out the fire of the enemy, it gives you the victory over the evil one.

Darts are spears or arrows, something that the enemy throws at you.

Fiery means burning, inflamed, or on fire.

To further elaborate (Ephesians 6:16), let us examine what happens in western movies (Cowboys & Indians). Guns, bows, and arrows are used as weapons. The arrows lit up, they were set on fire, and these flaming arrows were shot not at the individuals, but at the wagons to cause distraction.

Likewise, when Satan throws fiery darts at you, it is meant to cause distraction because when you are distracted you lose focus. So, you have to recognize him for what he truly is. Just as the wagons were set on fire to distract the enemy, the fiery darts are designed to distract you from your God-given assignment by chasing the fire. Don't be distracted from your God-given assignment. These distractions occur in your mind and often manifest in thoughts, words, attitudes, behavior, and fears. Know that when you are distracted, upset, and angry, then, as expected you are Inflamed.

This is why we need the shield of faith to protect us from the fiery darts of the enemy. The shield of faith protects our mind, hearts, body, finances, and anyone who is connected to us. Because Satan can attack you in any way and if he can't attack us directly, he will attack people close to us, he can attack your spouse and your family if you are married.

So, put on your shield of faith and get connected with fellow Christian believers with their shields of faith . This protects you from the enemy. Satan is desperate, and he will stop at nothing to attack you and anything and anyone close to you. Your shield of faith should be big enough to cover you, and others around you, because Satan is looking for a crack in your life to get in.

Now, let's get into the scriptures.

> When He had come to the other side, to the country of the Gergesenes, there met Him, two demon-possessed men, coming out of the tombs, exceedingly fierce, so that no one could pass that way. And suddenly they cried out, saying, "What have we to do with You, Jesus, You Son of God? Have you come here to torment us before the time?" (Matthew 8:28-29)

Satan will have you believe that demons and the demonic realm are not real. But that is a lie and a distraction from the absolute truth. The Word of God says Satan is real and that he comes to kill, steal, and destroy (John 10:10). He likes to take advantage of you. The Apostle Paul wrote in (2 Corinthians 2:11) that you should not be ignorant of the devices of Satan.

From (Matthew 8:28-29) we understand that Jesus Christ didn't introduce himself to the demons, but the demons knew exactly who Jesus was, that he was the Son of God. They were also aware of their ultimate doom which is eternal torment. Recall they asked Jesus Christ, 'have you come to torment us before our time?' This conversation points to the fact that demons know there is a set time for their destruction. Therefore, we need to connect with other believers so we can have our shield of faith on and be protected on every side. When we link up with other believers, and we all have our shield of faith on, we create a fortress and Satan can't get in, . When we come together collectively as the body of Christ with our shield of faith onthere is nothing the enemy can do to penetrate.

We Are On an Assignment from God

We have to understand that we are on assignment from God. The enemy will have you question yourself, your future, and God's plan for your life. He will make you doubt your assurances of salvation, particularly when you are going through tough times.

Whatever it is that you are going through, God can give you a breakthrough, I have seen several breakthroughs in my life when my mother was sick and the Doctors said she wasn't going to make it, I stood my ground and said that was a lie, she would live and not die and there is no way I am going to lose my mother. My mother got healed and the doctors couldn't explain it and my mother's recovery was a miracle. To have breakthroughs, you need to have faith and be connected to the right people. Everybody needs a breakthrough, at some point in their life. Whatever circumstance you are right now, God can give you a breakthrough.

Are you in need of a financial breakthrough? God can give you a breakthrough right now, or, you need a healing in your body? God can come through for you too. If you need to renew your mind, God can also come through for you. He is the God of breakthroughs. He is the God of a third chance, and He is the God of a fourth chance. He is a compassionate God and the God of mercy. In quenching the fiery darts of the enemy with your shield of faith, you have to realize that greater is he who is you than he who is in the world (1 John 4:4) and that you are more than a conqueror (Romans 8:35–37). If you are more than a conqueror, you don't even need to fight!

There are Two Types of Battles

There is a natural battle, which takes place in the flesh, and there is a supernatural battle against demonic spirits. God has given us victory overall. Remember, in spiritual warfare, it is not about the actual person, but, the spirit behind the person. Let us look into the word of God (Mark 5:1-10).

Then, they came to the other side of the sea, to the country of the Gadarenes. And, when He had come out of the boat, immediately, there met Him, out of the tombs, a man with an unclean spirit. This man had his dwelling among the tombs; and no one could bind him, not even with chains, because he had often been bound with shackles and chains. And the chains had been pulled apart by him, and the shackles broken in pieces; neither could anyone tame him. And always, night and day, he was in the mountains and in the tombs, crying out and cutting himself with stones. When he saw Jesus from afar, he ran and worshiped Him. And he cried out with a loud voice and said, "What have I to do with You, Jesus, Son of the Most High God? I implore You by God that You do not torment me." For He said to him, "Come out of the man, unclean spirit!" Then He asked him, "What is your name?" And he answered, saying, "My name is Legion; for we are many." Also, he begged Him earnestly that He would not send them out of the country. (Mark 5:1-10).

Whenever you see unclean spirits in the Bible that can be demons, the spirit of darkness, or demonic activities. Demonic spirits are powerful because they are supernatural. Understand this, supernatural could be of God or Satan. Just because somebody has some power or supernatural ability doesn't make him or her be of God's power. Satan has powers too.

So, how do you judge spirits? You judge them by their fruit (Matthew 7:16-20). These weird spirits can even be in the house of God. If they are, you have to prove what kind of fruits they produce. Are they individuals of character? Are they walking in love? Are they walking in joy? Are they walking in peace? Are they long-suffering? Are they kind? (Galatians 5:22-26). Because if they lack any of these, then they are contrary to God, and if they are contrary to God, it confirms what the scriptures said; that you will know them by their fruit.

Turning the examination on yourself, if you don't have the fruit of the spirit, you need to ask the Holy Spirit to help you in that area.

The key is, if you don't have the fruit of the spirit, you are oppressed by demonic forces. But because you are saved, you can't be possessed. When you are oppressed by wicked spirits, most of the time you are unaware of it. But, in this teaching, we are going to call them out.

We are familiar with children cutting their wrists; know that when children cut their wrists, it has nothing to do with emotions. But, they are under the influence of demonic spirits. You need to consistently pray for them, anoint them, and bring them under the covering of the Holy Spirit and the presence of God. You must recognize the activities of demonic spirits to properly deal with them.

Besides, know that demons exist not just in the Bible, but they do live among us. They need to be driven out because individuals needed to be set free. Observe in (Mark 5:1-10) that at one point, the man possessed by wicked spirits was talking and at other times, the demons were talking. Jesus Christ asked what is your name? The demon answered and said, "Legion, for we are many."

This brings to mind the complexity of the deliverance process. The deliverance process for some is like the onion with layers of demonic influences being pulled off. Realize, also, the deliverance is not total when the demons are kicked out and the place left clean and empty. Like the scriptures say, seven more wicked spirits could come in (Matthew 12:43-45 compare Luke 11:26). Suffice to say, in total deliverance you have to fill the space with the word of God.

Now that we understand demonic spirits are real, we need the shield of faith to be protected from these dark spirits. Let's look at some ways in which demonic spirits operate with some fiery darts of the enemy.

Common Demonic Attacks

Some familiar examples of fiery darts provided in the Bible are physical illness, mental impairment, and the spread of false doctrine.

1. **Bitterness** is the number one fiery dart that the enemy uses to attack Christians.

Bitterness and unforgiveness

Bitterness and unforgiveness are when you walk around offended and complaining about everything and everyone around you. Bitterness and unforgiveness can make you physically sick. When you visit the doctors, they can't figure out what is wrong. It could be dark spirits in action because you opened a crack, and they came in. Also, understand that spirits of infirmity have a right to enter and operate through bitterness. To get healed, you have to forgive. Forgiveness breaks the power of bitterness and unforgiveness. It yields the peaceable fruit of righteousness.

When you forgive, you are doing it for yourself (your health and well-being), you are doing it so you so can be free, and you are doing it so your mind won't be held hostage by evil spirits.

2. **Envy & Strife** - The second on this list is envy and strife. If you allow the spirit of bitterness and

unforgiveness to keep your mind captive, then you graduate to envy and strife, that is, you got more wicked spirits coming in. And, you must deal with them, if you thought bitterness and unforgiveness were difficult, now it is going to be more difficult.

Strife is a demonic spirit that should be avoided at all costs. If we let envy & strife stay in our hearts for any length of time, it opens the door to all types of negative energy leading to everything from sickness to financial disaster. Envy & strife is marked by contention, discord, quarreling, and violent disagreements. It is the spirit of division that results from anger. It comes from Satan, and it can destroy our lives if we allow it. The best way to resist envy & strif is to be aware of it and refuse to give the enemy the authority to use it in your life.

3. **Isolation** - The next one is isolation. With this one, you feel like you want to isolate yourself even if you are normally a social person, but for some reason, you don't want to talk to people and you don't want to be around people. This is the oppression of evil spirits and when these continue, the spirit of depression comes on you. You have to confess whatever it is so you can let it off your mind. But first, you must recognize what is going on in your mind because you will never conquer what you

won't confess. Get in the word of God and fight back with the word (sword of the spirit) and learn how to use the blood of Jesus Christ (Revelation 12:11) and lean not on your own understanding (Proverbs 3:5-18).

4. **Fear** – It is another familiar fiery dart of the enemy. You are always fearful, you are scared to go out by yourself, you are scared to get on the subway, and you are scared to fly or go on a cruise. Fear is a spirit and when you are paralyzed by the spirit of fear, you can't decide. Know that God has not given you the spirit of fear, but the spirit of power and love, and a sound mind. (2 Timothy 1:7) Understand also, that these feelings are going to come, but you have a responsibility to push them aside and get on with your life.

5. **Magnifying your faults** - This is another fiery dart of the enemy. When you magnify your faults, you become critical of others and say negative things about yourself and other people. Quit saying I am stupid; that is a cliché that keeps you in bondage. You know your words form your world, always find something good to say, and if you can't find it, then you must keep your mouth shut.

6. **Vain Imagination** – Don't speak and give the thoughts any life. Vain imagination is when your

thinking is not productive or fruitful, these are fearful thoughts, thoughts of defeat, and failure. The best way to see vain imagination is when you are about to do something, and suddenly, your mind is flooded with reasons it won't work. Then, you are confused. Eventually, you won't do anything.

But Apostle Paul showed us how to manage Vain Imagination and what to think in **(Philippians 4:8).**

Do you know that most of the things you fear don't exist? They only exist in your mental canvas. Another example on how to control vain imagination is seen in the books of 2 Corinthians.

> **Casting down arguments and every high thing that exalts itself against the knowledge of God, bringing every thought into captivity to the obedience of Christ (2 Corinthians 10:5)**

As you dwell in vain imagination it darkens your mind and hardens your heart towards the things of God, you become complacent and judgmental. You use sayings like, I don't care, and I can't be bothered. Beloved, understand that, although Satan is out to steal, kill, and destroy (John 10:10), God wants you to have a good life (Jeremiah 29:11 and John 10:10). He wants you to be fully persuaded like Sarah and Abraham (Romans 4:21 and

Hebrews 11:11) that the things God says in His word are true and that they are for your good. So, it doesn't matter what the situation is because your confidence is on the word of God.

SUMMARY

The death of Jesus Christ on the cross has defeated Satan and all of his demons. I am fully persuaded that faith is seeing the invisible, touching the intangible, believing the impossible, and moving forward as it is possible. God wants us to operate from the place of faith. Accordingly, I am going to share with you (Romans 8:38-39) to close this chapter.

> For I am persuaded that neither death nor life, nor angels nor principalities nor powers, nor things present nor things to come, nor height nor depth, nor any other created thing, shall be able to separate us from the love of God which is in Christ Jesus our Lord. (Romans 8:38-39)

As belivers, we have to be fully persuaded that nothing can separate us from the love of God. The devil often tries to tempt us using any tricks, driving fear in all sorts of dimensions, but what Jesus Christ did for us on the cross defeated Satan for all eternity.

When Jesus Christ got on that cross, he said it is finished. These words meant that everything required for your freedom was done. Our responsibility now is to learn how to walk in the victory and know Satan for whom and what he is. We have to recognize that there are two invisible spiritual kingdoms, the kingdom of God and the Kingdom of Satan. Finally, brethren, when Satan tempted Jesus Christ, how did He defeat him? With the word of God, Jesus said it is written (Matthew 4:4-10). Therefore, be prepared with the word of God and dressed with your shield of faith. When you are dressed like this, you can quench the fiery darts of the enemy.

CHAPTER FIVE

THE SHOES OF PEACE

WE ALREADY DISCUSSED THE two invisible spiritual kingdoms in the previous chapter, which are, the kingdom of God and the kingdom of Satan. We also discussed that there is a war going on between these two invisible spiritual kingdoms. More so, we recognize that when we are saved, by default we belong to the kingdom of God, and that automatically sets us on a collision course with the devil. Following this, we take our main focus to Ephesians 6:15 in this chapter.

> And having shod your feet with the preparation of the gospel of peace;

The Casualty of the Spiritual War

In these spiritual battles, we don't want to become casualties of war just because we were not careful enough to recognize that there is a war going on. As believers, we are at the center of this war, which makes it easy for us to walk in the victory that Jesus died for us to have. Knowing that there is a war going on, the scriptures teach us that this war is not against flesh and blood. This is to say, it is not a physical fight where we put on gloves or use our knuckle and punches like boxing, judo, Kung Fu, karate, and kickboxing, but a spiritual fight where we use our mouth to engage the enemy. So, the Christian life is spiritual warfare. But, we already won the VICTORY through Jesus Christ, which means that Satan is already defeated. Therefore, our attack against Satan is defensive. We are defending the VICTORY which was procured for us by Jesus Christ.

When you were not saved, the devil didn't bother you much because you were on his side, and he did not consider you an enemy. However, the moment you got saved, you changed sides, and right away, you became his enemy. Since then problems you never experienced when you were not saved started happening and you are like, what is going on here? When I never went to church, I did not have this situation, now I go to church, I am getting loads of problems. This happens because, by getting saved, you declared your allegiance to God and got enrolled in His army. That pitched you against the army of Satan. But, the good news is that Satan is already defeated, that is to say, you already won the battle against him.

The Shoes of peace according to (Ephesians 6:15). It is interesting, to see how the following three translations rendered this same Bible verse.

1. The New King James Version (NKJV) says, and having shod your feet with the preparation of the gospel of peace.

2. The New International Version (NIV) says, and with your feet fitted with the readiness that comes from the gospel of peace.

3. And New Living Translation (NLT) says, for shoes, put on the peace that comes from the Good News so that you will be fully prepared.

This is the sum of the believers warfare because we already have the victory. When you come from a place of victory as opposed to the place of defeat, you must have a victory mindset. On the contrary, if you have a defeated mindset, your whole attitude is different. This also applies to our health because the bible says, by his stripes, we are healed. (Isaiah 53:5 & 1st Peter 2:24).

You must recognize that we are not coming from a place of sickness; but, from a place of health. This means that we are not the sick seeking healing, but because we are already healed, we just need to walk into our divine health. Additionally, the word of God says let the weak say I am strong (Joel 3:10). This scripture suggests we are strong even if we feel weak in our bodies. We only need to walk in divine strength. As the scriptures said, let the weak say I am strong. The scriptures say, let the poor say I am rich because, though he was rich, yet for your sake, he became poor so that you, through His poverty, might become rich. (2 Corinthians 8:9).

Likewise, we need to walk into divine wealth as we are already rich. How do we walk into divine wealth? We walk into divine wealth through the blessings and favor of God. The favor of God is greater than anything you can ever imagine. The favor of God will open doors that no man can close. The favor of God creates jobs no one can create. This is why Satan is mad at us because he lost his ground - he cannot access God's favor, but we do.

The Preparation of the Gospel of Peace

The word Preparation is defined as the action or process of making ready or being made ready for use or consideration. The keywords are prepared and ready.

Are you preparing to be used of God?

The word readiness implies constant or consistent mindfulness.

Are you mindful of the things of God?

A Christian soldier must be prepared for battle. He/she must have a strategy and must have studied the enemy's strategy first. A Christian soldier is confident in his/her strategy. His/her feet must be securely grounded so that they could hold their ground when the enemy attacks. As a result, army war shoes were studded with spikes to help them keep their balance in battle.

I remember the **"Rumble in the Jungle"** how Muhammed Ali knocked out George Foreman, in the sixth round. When Muhammed was asked how this happened since George Foreman hasn't been knocked down before, Muhammed Ali said, "I studied him; I studied his strategy and knew he has never made it to the sixth round and I knew if I could hold on until the sixth round, I will knock him out" Likewise, we need to study the enemy's strategy. You can't keep falling for the enemy's trick every single time. The scriptures said we are not ignorant of the devices of the enemy (2 Corinthians 2:11). You need to sit down with the word of God to get a strategic plan on how to get rid of the enemy the next time he comes after you.

Having said that, the preparation of the gospel is two (2) fold.

Two (2) Fold Preparations

- First, The Gospel is a firm foundation on which Christians are to stand on.
- Second, Christian soldiers should be ready to go out to defend and or spread the Gospel.

As a Christian, you should be prepared to defend and, or spread the gospel. Knowing that we should be prepared, on what foundation are we to prepare? If I only go to church on Sundays, then I am ill-equipped for battle and can easily quit when Satan turns the heat on me. And, if I regularly attend Tuesday Bible studies and only learn the word and not practice it, I am just a hearer and not a doer of the word.

Flip-Flops and Proper Army Shoes

It is our responsibility to get a strategy that works for us. But, a lot of Christians don't want to put on their proper shoes of peace, they want to put on their flip-flops. Why would they put on flip-flops? Because they don't want to leave their comfort zones, the flip-flops are convenient and allow them to easily slip their foot in and out. They don't want to commit themselves, so they use the flip-flops. They forget that as Christians, they are in a battle and with the flip-flops on, they can easily slip or trip on the battlefield and become a casualty of war.

Stop wearing flip-flops and get the proper army shoes on.

For Christ, I Live, For Christ, I Die.

You have to be serious about your walk with God. Christianity is not always a life of comfort and convenience, but that of conviction and responsibility. You are a role model, and many are looking up to you. You cannot be careless because the enemy, like a roaring lion, seeks whom he may devour (1 Peter 5:8). Satan is a thief with a three-fold agenda; to kill, steal, and destroy. He tries to steal your joy; he tries to kill your dream and to destroy your business. Understand that salvation is real, and the devil will stop at nothing to destroy or rob you of it.

Accordingly, (2Timothy 2:15) says, *be diligent to present yourself approved to God, a worker who does not need to be ashamed, rightly dividing the word of truth.*

When we talk about being approved, it means what remains after being tested, because there will be testing. You will be tested for authenticity. Whether, you are an evangelist, pastor, or Apostle, you will be tested to validate your calling, ministry, or relationship with God.

Your walk with Christ will be tested for authenticity.

(Romans 10:14) says, how then shall they call on Him in whom they have not believed? And how shall they believe in Him of whom they have not heard? And how shall they hear without a preacher?

You are a preacher, whether you know it or not. When you got saved you became a preacher. Even if you never handled a microphone or stood on the pulpit, when you tell somebody you are a Christian you become a preacher. Everywhere you go, in everything you do, and in everything you say the world is watching. For some, you are the only preacher or sermon they can get access to. Your lifestyle is their message of salvation. They may never own a Bible or the opportunity to go to church but will have a sermon through you.

Be prepared as the soldier of Jesus Christ.

The armor is the military provision that is made by Jesus Christ for us, the soldiers of Jesus Christ. Not everyone is His soldier since not everyone will take responsibility. As usual, some will rather put on their flip-flops for convenience and stay in their comfort zones. They always have excuses for why they cannot be committed (Matthew 22:1-5) the Parable of the Wedding Banquet.

(Romans 10:15) says, and how shall they preach unless they are sent? As it is written: "How beautiful

**are the feet of those who preach the gospel of peace,
who bring glad tidings of good things.**

Preachers with the Beautiful Feet

Back in the Roman army time, they used to have messengers who will go and tell the people what was going on at the battlefield. When the messengers were coming, their feet sounded beautiful as they were bringing good tidings to the people from the war. When the messengers arrive the people would say, how beautiful are the feet of those who bring the news of good tidings. Likewise, as Christians, put on your shoes of the gospel of peace. The gospel of peace is about glad tidings; we need to always bring good news - the good news of salvation to the world. Letting them know they don't have to die as sinners because a way of escape has been made for them through Jesus Christ. Telling them the good news about their health because Jesus Christ took care of their sickness (Isaiah 53:5 & 1st Peter 2:24).

Jesus Christ Made Peace through His Blood Shed On The Cross

The Bible teaches that we all need the gospel of peace. Jesus Christ made Peace by his blood, shed on the cross. Still, many people, men, and women are searching for peace within, not knowing they must first have peace with God. Beloved, there is no way you will have peace within unless you have peace with God. If you don't have peace within, what you have is turmoil. You easily know the folks who have no peace within because of their tantrums and the sudden burst of fury. They are this way because they have not asked God for wisdom to handle their bad temper. The Bible said, let him that lack wisdom ask. God will always give you the wisdom that you seek when you ask.

When you recognize that you don't have peace, you need to go to God and ask for it. And because you have a relationship with Him, He will give you the peace that you seek. How do you develop your relationship with God? By putting on your shoes of the gospel of peace, to put on your shoes of the gospel of peace, you are required to walk in love, peace, kindness; otherwise known as the fruit of the spirit (Galatians 5:22-23)

Through studying the Bible, you understand that first, you need to have peace with God (Romans 5:1), which means to reconcile with Him. Reconciliation with God will open the door to the Peace of God within you. Then, you can enjoy peace with your sisters and brothers who have attained the same PEACE!!

Community Give-A-Way {Sister DEE's Story}

I was thinking about the community giveaway the other day. As we prepare for our community giveaway, we must keep at the forefront of our mind that the ultimate goal is to allow people to have a direct encounter with the true and living GOD through you.

At one of the giveaway events, Sister Dee was right there when we were sharing food. Just like everybody else, she was offered some food, and she said she didn't need any. She said she had no peace because her mother had just passed away, putting her in a very sorrowful state. So we Prayed with her that God would bless her with peace, and be strengthened to handle the mourning, pain, anxiety, and turmoil that came with the loss of her mother. Sister DEE needed an encounter with Jesus Christ. This experience summarized the key goal of the community giveaway. That is, to give people a direct encounter with the true and living God through us.

We need to be armed with the word to be able to give people a direct encounter with the true and living God.

The ABCs of The Good News (Gospel)

The simplest way to share the good news (Gospel) is by using the ABC acronym.

A - ADMIT. You must admit something, admit you are a sinner, so you can avoid death because the wages of sin is death. (Romans 6:23 & Romans 10:9)

B - BELIEVE. You must believe something. Believe Jesus Christ died for your sins, and he took your place so that he can save you and do the things he said he was going to do. (Acts 16:31 & Romans 10:9)

C - COME TO. You must come. You need to come to the open invitation of Jesus Christ. You should know him as your Lord and savior, as well as develop your relationship with him. And the last one is;

G – GO. You have to go preach the good news (gospel). (Isaiah 55:1-3 & Matthew 11:28-30).

As his children, we must get the message of salvation out there on the street to the hurting soul (Matthew 28:19). But are you prepared to go with the message? The preparation of the gospel of peace is to be prepared with the word of God. You need to be convinced of why you believe and what you believe before you can pass it on to somebody else. But a lot of us are stuck between our SIN and GO.

Stuck Between Sin and Go

We are stuck because we cannot deliver a message that we, ourselves don't believe. You need to be prepared; if you say I am a beliver, what makes you a Beliver ? Quit living in sin and get into the word of God to be prepared. However, be armed with the word of God, in case somebody needs salvation. Right away, you give them ABC (Admit, Believe, and Come).

Our primary goal, as belivers, is to get people on the Lord's side. The foundation for them is to have an encounter with the true and living God capsuled in the ABC acronym (Admit, Believe, and Come). When we read or speak the word and somebody has an encounter, the evidence is CHANGE.

Change the Evidence of Salvation

If you have an encounter with God, you can't stay the same. If you are, then you must be working hard to stay at your convenience. However, once you accept change and get transformed, the desire for the things of God becomes your nature and lifestyle. You get on with the things of God with less effort because the word now lives in you (John 15:7). In other words, you hide the word of God in your heart. (Psalm 119:11) says, *Your word I have hidden in my heart that I might not sin against you.* When an occasion comes and you need the word, the Holy Spirit brings it to your remembrance.

Are you thirsty?

On the last day, that great day of the feast, Jesus stood and cried out, saying, *"If, anyone thirsts, let him come to Me and drink. He who believes in Me, as the Scripture has said, out of his heart will flow rivers of living water." But this He spoke concerning the Spirit, whom those believing in Him would receive; for the*

Holy Spirit was not yet given because Jesus was not yet glorified. (John 7:37-39)

In these scriptures, Jesus Christ invites those who were thirsty. Though he was not yet glorified, he was going to satisfy their needs through the Holy Spirit. You have to be thirsty for God to have an encounter with His Word and the Holy Spirit. Sister DEE at the giveaaway was hungry for something with deeper satisfaction than food – an encounter. When you are hungry, your stomach growls, likewise, when your spirit is thirsty or hungry, he roars. How are you satisfying your spirit? With the WORD or with the WORLD?

The Promise of the Holy Spirit

When Jesus Christ finished his assignment on earth before he left for heaven, God through him, promised us a helper (John 7:37-39 & John 14:16-18, 26). Hence, the Holy Spirit was given to us as our helper. Although we sometimes confuse Him with speaking in tongues, he is not just speaking in tongues. Speaking in tongues is evidence that the Holy Spirit lives in us. When the Holy Spirit dwells in us, we have the power of the true and living God in us.

Understand that the Holy Spirit living in you is the same Holy Spirit responsible for the miracles which occurred in the Bible, he raised the dead (Acts 9:36-42), he was the one, the woman with an issue of blood encountered, and she was made whole (Mark 5:25-34), he was the one who shut the lion's mouth when Daniel was thrown into the lion's den (Daniel 6:22), he was the fourth man with Shadrach, Meshach, and Abednego (Daniel 3:24-26) when they were thrown into the furnace of fire.

The Book of Acts is a testimony of what the Holy Spirit could do among ordinary men and women who believed. And, because they stepped out in faith, healings, prophesying, raising of the dead to life, deliverance and supernatural encounters became part of their ministry so that they were able to take the gospel from Jerusalem to Samaria, to Asia Minor, to Africa, and Europe.

Yes, these demonstrations of the power of the Holy Spirit are all spectacular. But no less spectacular than character transformation that took place in lives that were yielded to the Holy Spirit's processing. Among the disciples, we see the dramatic transformation of a frightened, illiterate, rap-tag group to leaders with great boldness, tenacity, courage, compassion, wisdom, and passion to win souls, equipped with all the Spirit-led strategies needed to take the gospel to the ends of the earth. We, too, as we present ourselves to God as broken-vessels ready to be used for His purposes, can be confident He will use us, too.

Now, let's dig deeper into the word

And having shod your feet with the preparation of the gospel of peace; (Ephesians 6:15)

The word shod in this context, though unpopular in contemporary English vocabulary, is still being used in preparing the horseshoe to protect their feet. Horses that are used for racing and the ones used to pull extreme weight need shod on their feet to prevent their hooves from wearing. Horses also require shod on their feet to give them traction during snow and when they walk on ice. Similarly, in spiritual warfare, we can think of Christians having shod or wearing a footgear similar to the horseshoes. When our feet are shod with the preparation of the gospel of peace, they are protected. We may pick up nails and it wouldn't hurt us (Psalm 91:13; Luke 10:19).

When our feet are shod with the preparation of the gospel of peace, it gives us three different positions of defense and security - stability, mobility, and adaptability

Secured Positions When We Shod Our Feet with Shoes of Peace

To start with, let me give you a quick rundown of the three positions, stability, mobility, and adaptability.

Stability

This is the capacity to be stable, or state of being stable. It means to be firm, solid, steady, sturdy, secured, and safe. (Ephesians 6:10-18) instructs us to stand at least three times.

Verse 11 says to put on the whole armor of God that you may be able to stand against the wiles of the devil. Here, the wiles of the devil are the attacks of the devil which we already spoke about like his fiery darts.

Verse 13 says; therefore, take up the whole armor of God that you may be able to withstand in the evil day, and having done all, to stand. Here, the evil day represents those moments or times you are under the attacks of the evil one. When I think of standing in the evil day, I think about Job. Looking at (Job 1:13-22), you realize that he had his entire life and everything he owned; business, children, family, and health destroyed in one day – the evil day.

Verse 14 says, stand, therefore, having girded your waist with truth, having put on the breastplate of righteousness. You see from these scriptures on three different occasions, we were told to stand. We must not stumble because the attacks of the enemy will always come.

We have to stand when things are not the way we think they should be. We have to stand when the word of God is not popular. We have to stand when the facts are not lining up with the truth of the word of God. We have to stand now when a lot of things are not lining up with the word of God.

We have to know the word of God and we have to stand firm on it.

Mobility

This is the quality or state of being mobile. As Christian soldiers, we must be prepared to share the gospel of peace. That is telling the good news everywhere we go. Your lifestyle tells the gospel of peace whether you know it or not. So, be ready with the accurate knowledge of God's word that you can easily share with someone else because you can't give someone something that you don't have.

Concerning giving the gospel of peace, I was listening to somebody giving us a scenario of this lady at the grocery store. As the lady was about to pay for her groceries, she became anxious and nervous. It looked like she was having a nervous breakdown. This was a perfect opportunity to minister to her. If I was prepared with the gospel of peace, I could go to her right there and minister to her and help her to calm down. But, if I am not prepared, I will not be equipped with the word of God to speak peace (Shalom) into her life.

PS. Shalom = is a Hebrew word meaning peace, harmony, wholeness, completeness, prosperity, welfare, and tranquility and can be used to say hello and goodbye. What is significant about the word shalom that can actually give us 'peace' as we watch the world decay around us?

Peace or shalom is not the absence of conflict. True shalom is 'the destruction of the world's chaos by infusing the presence of God', the only presence that can destroy the 'one who causes the chaos'.

This is not a worldly battle fought with weapons of war. It's a spiritual battle for the soul's humanity. Souls: Mind, will, emotions & intellect.

She is having a nervous breakdown and she desperately needs the peace I have in me but, if you have your flip-flops on without the proper shoes, I would be missing an opportunity to help somebody. The gospel of peace is not restricted to the four walls of the church. It has to be mobile. We must have mobility in our shoes of peace. You must study the Word, memorize the word, and communicate the word. Mobility is all about motion, like Jesus Christ, we have to be about our father's business (Luke 2:49)

Bring the Good News of the Word of God into the Bad News World

Jesus Christ is the author of good news. No one else is qualified to save us, but JESUS (John 14:6; Acts 4:12).

When Jesus Christ sent out his disciples to preach the gospel of peace, he instructed as follows;

> And when you go into a household, greet it. If the household is worthy, let your peace come upon it. But if it is not worthy, let your peace return to you. (Matthew 10:12-13)

You have to have PEACE if you are going to give someone PEACE. Having your shoes of PEACE on means to be ready, so that people can experience your PEACE. However, the unfortunate experience is some of us have flip-flops on.

Adaptability

This is the quality of being able to adjust to new conditions. It means being flexible, versatile, compliance, and adjustable. God's calling upon our lives demands that we are flexible. We can't be so stiff doing everything the same way all the time. We must be adjustable, adaptable, and flexible to allow the move of the Holy Spirit. One of the books we have to go over in our discipleship is titled "Experiencing God." In this book, it says whenever we see God at work, we have to stop whatever we are doing and join Him.

A brilliant illustration is when you are on your way to an appointment, and before you, is somebody in need. You started to minister to this person, the time is 12:30, and your appointment is for 1:00, the time is now 12:45 you haven't finished yet. And, as you continue to minister, the time eventually gets to 12:55, and now it is 1:00, you have missed your appointment, you may say. But, if you are working with God you will discover later that the appointment was rescheduled. To be adaptable to the Holy Spirit, you have to be willing and compliant.

When you see God at work join him.

God's Word Does God's Work by God's Spirit

Yielding to the Holy Spirit comes with peace, joy, satisfaction and fulfillment. He'll work out everything around you perfectly. Finally, the adaptability of the gospel of peace is being a yielding vessel for God, always. You may not be privy to the several ways God wants to use you. So, there is no need for anxiety. You only need to be available and ready.

> (Philippians 4:6-7) says, be anxious for nothing, but in everything by prayer and supplication, with thanksgiving, let your requests be made known to God; and the peace of God, which surpasses all understanding, will guard your hearts and minds through Christ Jesus.

The Gift of the Holy Spirit and His Peace

> These things I have spoken to you while being pres-
> ent with you. But the Helper, the Holy Spirit, whom
> the Father will send in My name, He will teach you
> all things, and bring to your remembrance all things
> that I said to you. Peace I leave with you, My peace
> I give to you; not as the world gives do I give to you.
> Let not your heart be troubled, neither let it be afraid.
> You have heard Me say to you, 'I am going away and
> coming back to you.' If you loved Me, you would rejoice
> because I said, 'I am going to the Father,' for My Father
> is greater than I (John 14:25-28).

Jesus Christ, in the verses above, promised us the gift of
his peace through the Holy Spirit. The gospel of peace
is the message of salvation that Jesus Christ gives to
us when we trust in him. It is doing God's work with
God's spirit, no explanation is required. Listen to what
the Holy Spirit wants to say and say it. Then, allow the
Holy Spirit to do the work. You have no input because
you are just the messenger.

Preach the Word in Season And Out Of Season

> I charge you, therefore, before God and the Lord Jesus
> Christ, who will judge the living and the dead at His

appearing and His kingdom: Preach the word! Be ready in season and out of season. Convince, rebuke, exhort, with all longsuffering and teaching. For the time will come when they will not endure sound doctrine, but according to their own desires, because they have itching ears, they will heap up for themselves teachers; and they will turn their ears away from the truth, and be turned aside to fables. But you be watchful in all things, endure afflictions, do the work of an evangelist, fulfill your ministry (2nd Timothy 4:1-5).

The Shoes of Peace Have Two Purposes

We must recognize the gospel is not seasonal and the peace shoes God provides for us, as Christian soldiers have dual purposes: protecting and attacking. In defending ourselves against the fiery darts of Satan, we must be fully persuaded of our confidence in Jesus Christ. We must stand secured in the truth of God's word, regardless of how scary the situations may be (1 John 5:14). We must also, know that we have to preach the gospel of peace even if it is not comfortable. Preaching the gospel of peace is being on the offensive against Satan.

Confidence and Compassion in Prayer

Now, this is the confidence that we have in Him, that if we ask anything according to His will, He hears us. And if we know that He hears us, whatever we ask, we know that we have the petitions that we have asked of Him. (1st John 5:14-15).

As you sleep and ready to roll, be convinced that God will always provide the provisions you need even before you roll. Therefore, in making a request, through prayers, you ask with full assurance expecting His response.

Dead to Sin, Alive to God

What shall we say then? Shall we continue in sin that grace may abound? Certainly not! How shall we who died to sin live any longer in it? Or do you not know that as many of us as were baptized into Christ Jesus were baptized into His death? Therefore, we were buried with Him through baptism into death, that just as Christ was raised from the dead by the glory of the Father, even so, we also should walk in newness of life. For if we have been united together in the likeness of His death, certainly we also shall be in the likeness of His resurrection, knowing this, that our old man was crucified with Him, that the body of sin might be done away with, that we should no longer be slaves of sin. (Romans 6:1-6)

As believers, we are no longer slaves to sin. Therefore, we should abstain from sin and live above it. We are new creatures in Jesus Christ, old things have passed away (2nd Corinthians 5:17-21). We must, therefore, have our shoes of peace on and ready to roll without getting stuck between SIN and GO.

Having our shoes of peace on is the preparation that we need to get the gospel of salvation (the good news) out there to a hurting world.

In conclusion, (2Timothy 4:2) instructs us to preach the word and be ready in season and out of season. Therefore, be prepared to preach the gospel of peace and minister to a hurting world.

CHAPTER SIX

THE SWORD OF THE SPIRIT

IN THIS CHAPTER, I will teach about the Sword of the Spirit, which is the word of God. The Sword of the Spirit is one of the six pieces of the armor God - which He wants us to wear because we are in a spiritual battle.

> And the sword of the Spirit, which is the word of God;
> (Ephesians 6:17)

In the text above Apostle Paul identified the sword of the Spirit as the word of God, the spirit in this context is the Holy Spirit. This means that the word of God is the sword of the Holy Spirit. As believers, you need the word of God to be able to fight in spiritual battles. If you don't have the word of God in you, you are not equipped to fight spiritual battles. Knowing that if you don't have the word of God you cannot fight in a spiritual battle. It behooves you to first get the word of God in YOUR HEART. David said *Your word I have hidden in my heart, that I might not sin against You (Psalms 119:11).*

David knew that if he hid the word of God in his heart, he will not sin against God. In other words, he was saying the reason he will not sin against God is that the word of God lives in him. He will not sin against God because the word of God in him will quicken him and help him to do the things of God. Likewise, as Believers, when we have the word of God in us, the word will quicken us and help us to do the things which God wants us to do.

As we proceed in this teaching, understand that all the other pieces of armor we have studied are defensive weapons. But the sword of the Holy Spirit, which is the word of God, is an offensive weapon. In the armory of Christian warriors, there are two kinds of weapons, defensive and offensive weapons.

Defensive and Offensive

Knowing that the word of God is an offensive weapon, let's define these two unique positions in the Christian believer's warfare. The offensive is to be actively and aggressively attacking the enemy by using the word of God. And, defensive is the act of defending or resisting an attack. (Hold off the enemy).

In the church, however, I observed a lot of Believers don't know the word of God. And, the majority of Christians go to church because the church is what we do on Sunday morning.

If you don't have the word of God in your heart, you are just going through the motions and your Christian life is just a ceremony. Perhaps, the reason the enemy is assaulting you with every opportunity he has is that you don't have the word of God in you. As a new Christian believer, it is acceptable to ask some other brethren to pray for you because you are relying on their God, and depending on their relationship with God to help you. But there comes a time in your Christian journey when you need to develop your personal relationship with God and be matured in handling the things of God.

Now that we understand in spiritual warfare there is an offensive and a defensive weapon and that the word of God is an offensive weapon, you have to be disciplined enough to know the word of God. Anybody can memorize the word of God, that is acceptable, but you cannot use memorized scriptures in spiritual warfare. It is only the scriptures in your heart you can call up when you need them

As Believers, it is not sufficient to know the word and not practice it. The scriptures say, *take the sword of the Spirit, which is the word of God; (Ephesians 4:17),* and in John, *the Helper, the Holy Spirit, whom the Father will send in My name, He will teach you all things, and bring to your remembrance all things that I said to you. (John 14:26)*

From these scriptures, the Holy Spirit will teach you all things and will bring all things to your remembrance. If, you haven't read the word of God, what will the Holy Spirit bring to your remembrance? The Holy Spirit can only bring to your remembrance what you know. He cannot bring the word you don't know to your remembrance.

You can only remember something you know or have been exposed to. You can't remember what you don't know.

There was a time I had a difficult day at work, my heart was heavy because of the things that were said. When I came into the church for prayers, I sat at the altar talking to God about what happened, and, as I was there talking to God, I heard God speak to me clearly, "I gave you that job." As soon as I heard those words, my heart was lifted, and my tears dried up. The joy of the Lord filled my heart. I wasn't concerned about the job anymore and it didn't matter what they were doing and what they were saying, because I knew that God gave me that job. I was convinced!

You must hold on to the word the Lord gave you during trials, persecutions, and tribulations. If the Lord gave you the word, the word is true no matter your circumstances and will come to pass. The word of God is always true, and valid regardless of the situation.

I am sure you have received a word from the Lord. If you have and the word is not yet fulfilled in your life, hold on to it, it will surely come to pass. For in the due season, if you faint not it will come to pass (Galatians 6:9). Sometimes, you have to go through some experiences to be prepared and get ready for the word to come to pass in your life. God won't give you anything before you can handle it.

For more ideas on the word of God let's go to Hebrew 4:12, In Hebrews 4:12 God says,

> For the word of God is living and powerful, and sharper than any two-edged sword, piercing even to the division of soul and spirit, and of joints and marrow, and is a discerner of the thoughts and intents of the heart.

The scriptures above talk about the word of God and the power of the word to transform the Christian believer. Once you begin to study the word of God and the word get settled in, that is when your mind starts to transform. Then, you want to do the things that the word of God is calling you to do. Keep in mind that, until your mind is transformed, you will do the things the world will always have you do. But, when you have the word, it will quicken your spirit and help you to do the things of God.

The word of God is a discerner of your thought and the intent of your heart.

We Are a Triune Being

We live in a body, we have a soul and we are a spirit. That is, we are a spirit being having a human experience. The Spirit being is awaken when we get saved. But we have the soul, which is the mind, will, emotions, and the intellect which tells us what to do. We are body, soul and spirit all at the same time. Our triune existence is not easy to explained or understand. The word of God can discern between our body, soul, and spirit.

Contrasting Hebrew 4:12 (NKJV) with the (AMPC)

For the Word that God speaks is alive and full of power [making it active, operative, energizing, and effective]; it is sharper than any two-edged sword, penetrating to the dividing line of the breath of life (soul) and [the immortal] spirit, and of joints and marrow [of the deepest parts of our nature], exposing and sifting and analyzing and judging the very thoughts and purposes of the heart. (AMPC)

The word of God is the measuring stick for judgment. God's message is alive and active, penetrating the innermost parts of a person. Knowing what is natural and what is spiritual, exposing your thought and intents. In addition, your motivation and intention will also be judged by the word of God. (NKJV)

Sometimes, we can do things that are not consistent with the word of God. But, understand that God knows the intent of the heart. He cannot be deceived. God knows the state of your heart. He knows the purity and sincerity of your heart. You may come to church and sit all day, but God knows those who are real and those who are doing it to get attention.

He knows when you are performing and doing everything you could, to draw attention to yourself and not to him.

Knowing that our thoughts can be examined by the word of God, you have to get it right to be able to glorify God in your thoughts. You also need to watch the things you say about your brethren. They may not hear you, but make no mistake, God heard you. Because you are a role model, a lot of people are watching you, perhaps, to see whether your God could be their God. Remember, because you are created in the image and likeness of God, you have to be pure and true because God is pure, and He is true.

As you profess Jesus Christ as your Lord and savior, the world is watching every single thing you do and every single step you take. They are watching how you respond to trials. They are looking for the light inside of you and thinking, maybe I need that kind of light. Some are lost watching to see if your way is the right way. Others are in pain, sad and depressed, and when the world is coming down on everyone else, they are waiting to see how you react.

And your reaction is as the songwriter wrote;
"I can't stop praising his name"

Jesus Christ is our model. We have to search the scriptures to see how Jesus Christ controlled trials, temptation, tribulations, and persecutions. Jesus Christ became flesh to have the same experiences as we have. Nothing happens or is going to happen to you that Jesus Christ hasn't experienced. No matter the situation you are going through, Jesus Christ has been there.

Jesus Christ Is Our Example

Get in the scriptures and discover what he did. There is power in the word of God. When we understand Jesus Christ as our example we need to find out what he did when the enemy came to tempt him. Whatever he did when Satan came to tempt him, that is exactly what we are supposed to do when the enemy is after us. We should follow the example of Jesus Christ. When the devil came to tempt him, he fought back with the word of GOD.

The devil tempted our Lord and Savior, Jesus Christ, three different times. Let's see how he responded. And for this, let's go to the book of Mathew.

Satan Tempts Jesus Christ

> Then Jesus Christ was led up by the Spirit into the wilderness to be tempted by the devil. And when He had fasted forty days and forty nights, afterward He was hungry. Now when the tempter came to Him, he said, "If You are the Son of God, command that these stones become bread." But He answered and said, "It is written, 'Man shall not live by bread alone, but by every word that proceeds from the mouth of God. (Matthew 4:1- 4)

When Satan tempted Jesus Christ, what was his weapon? The word of God! We also must arm ourselves with the accurate word of God and know how and when to use it against Satan. Understand, in verse 2, Jesus Christ was on a fast for forty days and hadn't eaten anything.

He just ended the fast and was hungry. Satan showed up telling him, now that he is hungry, he can turn stones into bread, so he can have something to eat.

But Jesus Christ shut the devil down with the word of God, reminding the devil that it is written in the word of God that men must not live by bread alone (Deuteronomy 8:3)

Jesus Christ fought the devil with "it is written" the scripture says if you resist the devil he will flee (James 4:7). He fled, but came right back, note the devil is persistent.

Then the devil took Him up into the holy city, set Him on the pinnacle of the temple, and said to Him, "If You are the Son of God, throw Yourself down. For it is written: 'He shall give His angels charge over you,' and, 'In their hands, they shall bear you up, Lest you dash your foot against a stone.'" Jesus Christ said to him, "It is written again, 'You shall not tempt the Lord your God.' (Matthew 4: 5-7)

Like I said earlier, Satan knows the scriptures. He quoted Psalm 91:11-12.

But Jesus Christ reminded him again, it's written. Jesus Christ knew Satan cannot get him to do the things God hasn't asked him to. Also, if somebody tries to get you off your sways, you have to know where your sways are because if you don't you will walk right into their traps. God has given us the word we needed for every situation. Some people will always come to you with suggestions that look good on the surface, but they are contrary to the word of God. During such times, you must stand your ground letting them know what your square is, and that you are crystal clear on what your square is.

More so, you must know what your square is and what God is called you to do. You have to know what line or frequency you are supposed to be on, so you can be in tune with God. When Satan tempted Jesus Christ, he resisted him with the word of God. And that is the second time Satan came to tempt Jesus Christ. He won't go away. Here he comes again the third time. He is persistent.

> Again, the devil took Him up on an exceedingly high mountain and showed Him all the kingdoms of the world and their glory. And he said to Him, "All these things I will give You if You will fall down and worship me." Then Jesus Christ said to him, "Away with you, Satan! For it is written, 'You shall worship the Lord your God, and Him only you shall serve.' Then the devil left Him, and behold, angels came and ministered to Him. (Matthew 4:8-11)

Three times, the devil tempted Jesus Christ with some mess, some Shenanigans, and Jesus Christ fought back with the word.

Have you observed that folks who want to mess you up are sadly the most persistent? THE DEVIL KNOWS MORE WORDS THAN MOST OF THE CHRISTIAN BELIEVERS. THE PROBLEM IS HE JUST COULD NOT LIVE IT. Many people know the word but can't live the word.

As, Believers we have a responsibility to; Know The Word, Believe The Word, And Live the Word!

When the enemy tries to come and get you, you must have the word of God ready to stand on. The word of God is the sword of the spirit. Whatever situation you are going through; you need to search the scriptures for the exact word you need to combat whatever it is the enemy is throwing at you. The devil is constantly whispering things in our ear.

A classical illustration is when he keeps telling you that you are not good enough, you are not a good parent, you are not beautiful, you are too fat, and your ears are too big. You have to silent the devil by letting him know, it is written in the word of God that you are fearfully and wonderfully made (Psalm 139:14), that you are the image and likeness of God (Genesis 1:26-27).

Your fists and your muscles are not going to help you fight the enemy. It is only through the word of God that you can fight the enemy. Note also, that if you fight the devil with worldly weapons you will be trapped because he has the mastery better than you. The only weapon the devil cannot gain the mastery at is the living word of God. So, why not get more and more of the living word of God? The word of God is never too much. The more you have the better.

Jesus Christ fought the devil with the word of GOD. If, Jesus Christ is our example how should we fight the devil? We fight the devil with the word of God.

As we go through the scriptures, we recognize that there are two kinds of words the Holy Bible represents, namely, Logos and Rhema.

Logos & Rhema

The Logos refer to the written word of God. That is the recordings of the Holy Bible are considered the logos. Logos, in the Greek term, translated in the English language as "word," "speech," "principle," or "thought."

Some people think that having a Holy Bible without knowing what it says will help them. So they put the Holy Bible in their car, under their pillow, by the side of their bed, and in their handbag. Beloved, if the word must be relevant in your life you have to open that Holy Bible, read the Holy Bible, study the Holy Bible, and use the Holy Bible in your daily life. I say this because the Holy Bible you don't know isn't going to help you. If you have your Holy Bible in your bookstand it remains in your rack and not in your heart. You need to pull that Holy Bible from the shelf and put the word in your heart.

The Logos represent the message of Jesus Christ and The Holy Bible.

Rhema

The Rhema is the word of God that is personal to you. You have the message of Jesus Christ in the Holy Bible, that is the logos, and you have the message that came out of the Holy Bible to you, which is personal to you. That is Rhema. The Rhema word can come from the written word, it can come from the preached word, and it can come from something you heard that will trigger the word of God in you. It is specific. Let's get an example of the Rhema word of God from the Holy Bible.

> And the angel answered and said to her, "The Holy Spirit will come upon you, and the power of the Highest will overshadow you; therefore, also, that Holy One who is to be born will be called the Son of God. Now indeed, Elizabeth your relative has also conceived a son in her old age; and this is now the sixth month for her who was called barren. For with God nothing will be impossible." Then Mary said, "Behold the maidservant of the Lord! Let it be to me according to your word." And the angel departed from her (Luke 1:35-38).

In this example, Mary, the mother of Jesus Christ received a message (prophecy) from the angel that she was going to be the mother of Jesus Christ. She got a Rhema word from the angel about her situation. Receiving the word and getting the manifestation of the word is the Rhema. When she heard the word from the angel that was the logos and when she received and believed the word, the word became personal to her. That word became Rhema to her.

The majority of you reading this book have received the word, a message, or a prophecy from God. If you have received a word, is it just logos? When you received the word of God, you have to make the necessary steps for that word to become your Rhema word. By the necessary steps, I don't mean you will make that word happen. God will make the word happen. But, you have to get yourself in the position where God can bring His word concerning you to pass. For instance, if you received a word to become a pastor, you are required first to spend time with God in his word preparing yourself.

For every word of God that you received, there is a piece that you have to do yourself. When the angel from the Lord gave that prophecy, Mary could have rejected it. But she confirmed the word by saying; *"Behold the maidservant of the Lord! Let it be to me according to your word,"* (Luke 1:38). When you have the understanding of the Rhema word of God, you know you are never sick because you always come from a place of healing.

When you have the Rhema word of God, you know are never poor, because you always come from the place of prosperity. But, if you haven't received the Rhema word of God, that is a different story altogether. When you have the Rhema word of God, even if your present situation doesn't look like it, Don't start complaining, hold on to that word by saying it even in the face of that circumstances. By speaking those words, you give life to them.

The power of life and death lies in your tongue (Proverbs 18:21). You need to prophesy to yourself speaking those things that be not as though they were (Romans 4:17). Until you see the manifestations of the things you are speaking.

Never Say What You See. But, Speak What You Want to See

As you say what you want to see you will have the manifestation of the things that you are saying.

Remember faith without work is dead (James 2:26).

Jesus Christ Is The Eternal Word Of God

In the beginning, was the Word, and the Word was with God, and the Word was God. He was in the beginning with God. All things were made through Him, and without Him, nothing was made that was made. In Him was life, and the life was the light of men. And the light shines in the darkness, and the darkness did not comprehend it. There was a man sent from God, whose name was John. This man came for a witness, to bear witness of the Light that all through him might believe. He was not that Light but was sent to bear witness of that Light. That was the true Light which gives light to every man coming into the world. He was in the world, and the world was made through Him, and the world did not know Him. He came to His own, and His own did not receive Him. But as many as received Him, to them He gave the right to become children of God, to those who believe in His name: who were born, not of blood, nor of the will of the flesh, nor of the will of man, but of God. And the Word became flesh and dwelt among us, and we beheld His glory, the glory as of the only begotten of the Father, full of grace and truth. (John 1:1-14)

From the scriptures above, it is clear that the "Word" or Logos is a reference to Jesus Christ.

And the Word became flesh and dwell among us. (John 1:14)

We need to have the understanding that the word is God. I hear some Believers say I have never received a word from God; I have never received a prophecy. Here is my suggestion, read the scriptures (the Holy Bible) out loud to your hearing that is the word of God and that is your prophecy. The truth is if you don't believe the Holy Bible, you are not going to believe anyone who comes to tell you something about God. God is the Word!

Jesus Christ is a triune being like us. We have a soul, spirit, and body. Equally, we have God the Father, God the Son (Jesus Christ), and God the Holy Spirit. When we study the word of God, the Old Testament educates us on whom God the Father is. Then, we came to the New Testament,it teaches us about Jesus Christ, the son of God, and the promises of salvation. Now we are the 67th book of the Holy Bible. (Recall the Holy Bible is made up of 66 books. 39 books in the Old Testament and 27 books in the New Testament).

You Are The 67th Book of The Holy Bible The Testament Of The Holy Spirit.

Recognize that you are the 67th book of the Holy Bible, the current and most recent epistle to the hurting world. Therefore, you are still being written. And, if you are the 67th book, you have to understand that people are reading you. Besides, as Christian believers, we need to recognize that we are in the dispensation of the Holy Spirit. We currently don't have a book about it because as stated earlier, we are writing it right now. God the Father in the Old Testament, Jesus Christ is the New Testament, and we are the testament of the Holy Spirit. Amen!!.

The Holy Bible says greater works shall we do (John 14:12). If Jesus Christ raised somebody from the dead, we should be able to resurrect the dead as well. If Jesus Christ healed the blind, it should be simple for us to heal the blind too. If Jesus Christ performed miracles, it shouldn't be difficult for us to do miracles. But why are we not seeing miracles? Because we don't believe the word, we are not speaking things into life. Speak those things you were told into existence.

We know from the scriptures that signs, wonders, and miracles shall follow them who believe (Mark 16:17). We as believers shouldn't be chasing after signs, wonders, and miracles because we are the custodian of signs, wonders, and miracles. People out there in the world should come to us for signs, wonders, and miracles. We shouldn't be running after signs and wonders and miracles, because they are supposed to be the believer's mark of identification. The visual and usual way to know a believer is because signs and wonders always trail them. Therefore, you have to know who you are, walking in dominion, power, boldness, in the Holy Spirit, and authority, demonstrating signs, wonders, and miracles.

Created For His Purpose

Recalling (John 1:1-14), the word is God and everything created was created for his purpose. He created you for his purpose, not for your purpose. So, you have to live for his purpose. For instance, a vacuum cleaner was created to keep the floor clean, what will happen when the vacuum cleaner decides to become a dishwasher. The vacuum cleaner will malfunction because it was not designed to wash dishes. Knowing that God created you for his purpose, it behooves you to find out what that purpose is.

"LORD WHAT DID YOU CREATE ME FOR?" stop asking this question right now and have a conversation with the Holy Spirit about your Divine Purpose.

He created you in a certain way to fulfill his purpose, and He created another in a certain way for his purpose, so learn to love your brethren the way they are because that is how God created them to serve his purpose and not your purpose. The vacuum cleaner trying to wash dishes will always breakdown. Likewise, if you do the things you are not created to do, you will breakdown. If you were created to be a praise singer and you wanted to be a pastor, you will flop. If you are called to be an intercessor and you wanted to be a preacher you will fail. If you were called to be a teacher and you wanted to an evangelist you will blip. And finally, if God called you to be a minister of the gospel and you wanted to be a minister of finance you will collapse.

Know what God called you to do. Therefore, walk in what God had called you to do.

Summary

Jesus Christ Is the Eternal Word of God

In this summary, I want to bring out 6 points from John's use of the Logos concept.

1. (John 1: 1) Jesus Christ is eternal (In the beginning was the Word)
2. (John 1: 1) Jesus Christ was with God prior to coming to earth (the Word was with God)
3. (John 1: 1) Jesus Christ is God (the Word was God)
4. (John 1: 3) Jesus Christ is Creator (All things were made through him)
5. (John 1: 4) Jesus Christ is the Giver of Life (In him was life)
6. (John 1: 14) Jesus Christ became human to live among us (the Word became flesh and dwelt among us)

That is the Rhema word. Jesus Christ became the living, breathing, walking, and working word of God. And He expects you to be the living, breathing, walking, and working word of God.

The opening of John's Gospel carries a striking resemblance to Genesis 1:1.

In the beginning, God created the heavens and the earth (Genesis 1:1)

In the beginning, was the Word, and the Word was with God, and the Word was God. He was in the beginning with God. All things were made through him (John 1:1).

From this study, we need to understand that the word of God is the sword of the Holy Spirit.

In retrospect, we established from (Ephesians 6:14-18) what the weapons of the Christian warfare are,

- The sword of the spirit is the Holy Spirit
- The belt of truth is the truth of the word of God
- The breastplate of righteousness is protecting your heart
- Preparation with the gospel of peace is walking in peace
- The shield of faith is your faith
- The Helmet of salvation is your salvation
- Finally, the ultimate weapon is prayers.

CHAPTER SEVEN

THE ULTIMATE WEAPON IS PRAYERS

Praying always with all prayer and supplication in the Spirit, being watchful to this end with all perseverance and supplication for all the saints (Ephesians 6:18).

S o, THIS CHAPTER MARKS the end of this book, but the Trilogy series continues. In the next book, we will be looking at prayer as a weapon that every beliver should be armed with. Nevertheless, we continue with this book's business, and, I like us to do a quick review of our teachings on the armor. (Ephesians 6:10-18).

(Ephesians 6:10) - Finally, my brethren, be strong in the Lord and in the power of His might.

This verse advised us to be strong in the Lord and the power of his might. Fighting spiritual battles is not what we can do with our ability. But, what the Lord God Almighty can do. Also, understand that we cannot use our physical strength to fight in the spiritual battle.

(Ephesians 6:11) - Put on the whole armor of God that you may be able to stand against the wiles of the devil.

Here, we are asked to put on the whole armor of God to be able to withstand the tricks of the devil. The wiles of the devils are his deceits, he comes into your mind to tell you things like, you cannot make it, you are not good enough, you are not beautiful, and you are a waste of space. The wiles of the devil also mean when he whispers things in your ears that are false and when he sets up event after event to keep you distracted depressed and frustrated like the case of Job (Job 1:13-22). These are some of the wiles or craftiness of the devil; understand the Apostle Paul referred to them as wiles to let us know they are not real.

(Ephesians 6:12) - For we do not wrestle against flesh and blood, but against principalities, against powers, against the rulers of the darkness of this age, against spiritual hosts of wickedness in the heavenly places.

We are not wrestling against flesh and blood, fighting with your sister, brother, friends, colleagues, your boss, or your pastor. You are wrestling with the spirit that is behind what any of these people might be doing to you. Understand the devil can inspire somebody to come against you, and you wouldn't even know (Psalm 35:15).

In retrospect, we established in this book that there are two invisible spiritual kingdoms, the kingdom God and the kingdom of Satan. And that these two kingdoms are in a perpetual war. If you profess Jesus Christ as your Lord and savior, by default, you are on the Lord's side. Accordingly, the enemy is going to come against you, because you are his enemy whether you chose it or not. And if you don't prepare yourself, you become a casualty of war. We don't want to become casualties of war, so, we equipped ourselves with the information to fight, the good fight of faith.

We understand , that we do not fight against flesh and blood but invisible spiritual forces. And the first of these unseen spiritual enemies are principalities. Principalities are ranked demons. Like we have in the regular army there are ranks, such as general, captain, major, and sergeant, you know the list, likewise, demons are ranked.

Like Christians, ranked demons and people that are possessed by the devil have powers. You don't have to panic, because the Bible states greater is he that is in you than he that is in the world (1 John 4:4) that is the power inside of you is greater than the power that is out there in the world. The next line says the ruler of the darkness of this age.

The rulers of the darkness of this age are like a dark cloud that controls the atmosphere over a certain region. Know that every phase in history has different powers of darkness that tries to rule. The next enemies Apostle Paul spoke about are the spiritual host of darkness in heavenly places. I have folks claim that the devil and his demons are in Hades, well, be informed, that the devil and his demons are not in hell. There are three levels of heaven, namely; the first level, the second, and the third level (2 Corinthians 12).

God lives on the third level. Remember also, when Daniel prayed (Daniel 10:13-21) the angel with the answers to his prayers was held for 21 days in the second heaven by the prince of Persia when the angel got to Daniel, he said your prayers were heard the first day, but he was caught up by the Prince of Persia, I had to fight my way, to come to you, but, because they too strong for me, I couldn't overcome them. However, angel Michael came and supported me, so I was able to come and deliver your message.

Understand that, in this discussion, the angel left the third heaven, he had to cross through the second heaven to get to the first heaven which is the atmosphere to get to Daniel. But, he was held in the second heaven. Know that the spiritual host of wickedness is in heavenly places. They operate between the first and the second heaven.

Effectively, in (Ephesians 6:13-17), the apostle Paul was telling us to put on the whole armor of God, what this armor is, and how to put on the armor of God. There are three pieces of armor we have to put on and there are three pieces of armor we have to take up as seen below.

Armors to Put On
- The belt of truth,
- The breastplate of righteousness, and
- The shoes of the gospel of peace

Armors to Take Up
- The shield of faith,
- The helmet of salvation, and
- The sword of the Spirit, which is the word of God

The reality is we should NEVER take it off or put it Down.

This brings us to the ultimate weapon of our spiritual warfare which is Prayer.

The only way prescribed for us by which we can win in this fight is through Prayer. Prayers are the only way we win our spiritual battles. Once you have your whole armor on, the ultimate weapon is to be able to pray.

> Praying always with all prayer and supplication in the Spirit, being watchful to this end with all perseverance and supplication for all the saints (Ephesians 6:18.)

The kingdom of heaven can only invade earth through the mechanism of prayer. Consequently, if you cannot pray about your situation God cannot intervene. Prayer is mandatory and not an optional spiritual weapon. You must know how to pray. Prayers involve petitioning God about the things you seek.

Let's go back to (Ephesians 6:18), *praying always with all prayer and supplication in the Spirit, being watchful to this end with all perseverance and supplication for all the saints.*

There are two keywords in the scriptures above, perseverance, and supplication. Now, let's examine the definitions of these important words are as follows;

Supplication is the action of appealing for or asking for something earnestly or humbly.

Perseverance is doing something to achieve success despite delays or difficulties. That is if you ask and it was not done, you have to ask again, the sequence continues until your petition is granted.

Know that if we are seeking, prayer is the only way to directly access God.

> Then God said, "Let Us make man in Our image, according to Our likeness; let them have dominion over the fish of the sea, over the birds of the air, and over the cattle, over all the earth and over every creeping thing that creeps on the earth." (Genesis 1:26)

Dominion in this context or usage means control. God has given us dominion, authority, and control. So, if, we don't take dominion, the whole world will be in disorder. Little wonder, there are so many crunches in our modern world because Christians are not doing what they should be doing taken control of the earth on behalf of heaven.

Furthermore, in the passage, we just read God said "let us make the man" who were these us? The "us" represents God the Father, God the Son, and God the Holy Spirit, the Holy Spirit dwells inside of you. God has given you authority over the whole earth. Taking dominion is you asking God, through prayers, to intervene in the situation on earth. Things are what they are and the world is what it is right now because Christian believers are not taking dominion. If you need or want God's help, you must ask him. God knows what your situation is; God knows what you are going through, God knows what you are up against. But he will not and cannot get involved until you ask him to.

Elijah prayed that there should be no rain, there was no rain. If Christians leaders can get on their knees asking God like Elijah (1 Kings 17) and Daniel (Daniel 10) to intervene in our world system instead of acquiescing to the world standard, there will be divine intervention. Understand that the same power that Elijah had you have. For three and a half years, Elijah declared a drought, he prayed again for rain and there was rain. If Elijah prayed for drought and rain and God heard him, we can pray for whatever it is and get results as well. Elijah was in expectation with full assurance (absolute conviction) of God's commitment to validate the course he has chosen on behalf of God's Kingdom.

Are you in the expectation that God is going to do what you had asked him to do? Are you convinced that God is going to confirm his word with signs and wonder through you? (Mark 16:20) Are you fully persuaded that God is committed to performing all that concerns you? Abraham was convinced (Romans 4:21).

Are you convinced?

If you are not in expectation, then there will be no application, and as a result, there will be no manifestation. So, are you in expectation? We have to be in expectation, behaving, and moving like it is already done. Thus, the way we get heaven to intervene in the affairs on earth is through faith in prayers and praying.

You Have To Ask In Prayer!!

Are you asking?

As we are praying for God's will, we have to understand two things as it relates to God's will. The first is God's conditional will, and the second is God's unconditional will. If you are praying in God's conditional will, the manifestation will always happen. Nonetheless, in my relationship and fellowship with God as a minister of His word, I have learned three answers from God when you pray in His conditional will. These answers are; "yes, no, and not right now". Therefore, when you pray, you have to find out what is God saying.

- Is He saying yes because it is time?
- Is He saying no because it is not yet time, or
- Is He saying wait because He wants you to focus on something else?

An example of the conditional will of God is it is God's will for all men to be saved. However, it is conditioned on acceptance by the unsaved. Thus, if the unbeliever refuses to do their part to accept the message of salvation, God's will for salvation, won't come to pass in such individuals.

An example of the unconditional will of God is that

God loves everybody, regardless of who you are, what you have been through, or where you are. God loves you. Furthermore, under God's conditional will, if He called you to be a pastor, and you don't take time to develop and train yourself in the word with the help of the Holy Spirit. God's will, for you as a preacher won't be fulfilled.

In doing God's will, we have to be cautious of the world's way of doing things. The world's way of doing things is making sure everything is right, even though you know there is no way you can be sure everything is right without God. On the contrary, in God's order, He gets you in motion. As you start moving, He begins to release instructions. He will tell you where to go, what to do, and how to. He wants you to say yes Lord, He wants us to yield, and step out in faith doing what He asked you to do. We are not going to understand the details. We have to act in obedience. Knowing that God's will is conditional and unconditional, we have to recognize the ultimate weapon for our spiritual battles is prayer.

Prayer is an earthly license for heavenly interference.

Now, let's do a recap, to get results from your prayers you have to pray for God's will. God's will is His Eternal Word. God's will come in two variants; the conditional will of God and the unconditional will of God.

The conditional will of God are subject to requirements being met. The unconditional will of God is not subject to any conditions.

Examples of these are:

- God's will is for all men to be saved is conditional
- God's love for humanity is unconditional

The Ultimate Weapon For Fighting Spiritual Warfare Is Prayer

I said earlier prayer is an earthly license for heavenly interference. To this end, there are four aspects of prayers we have to engage in. They are as follows;

- Praying always with all prayer
- Supplication in the Spirit,
- Being watchful to this end with all perseverance
- Supplication for all the saints

Prayer is our earthly license for heavenly interference that creates "MOMENTUM" for the spiritual progress of the Christian believer. Prayer is a compulsory spiritual requirement, and it is not voluntary. Prayers involve your vocal system; it has to be audible, not always quiet or silent. The effective and effectual prayers of the righteous avail much, when the prayers involve the whole of your being.

You need to open your mouth and speak the word of God. The scriptures say, let the redeemed of the Lord say so (Psalm 107:2).

Prayers develop from the mind, but, you can't just think it in your mind without saying it out with your mouth. The Bible says with the heart we believe but, with the mouth, we confess (Romans 10:9-10). Prayer in your mind is just a thought, like the several other thoughts you may have. Thinking about it is not the same as praying about it. You have to give voice to the word of God. It is through that speaking you engage angels on assignments. On the other hand, when you are not speaking you are giving the devil the right to do whatever they want to do.

When you are not speaking the truth, and you are speaking life, you authorize demons to have the rule over your life. Thus, you create a crack in your faith. When you open the crack in your faith by not speaking, the enemy will come in and strike. Know that the Holy Spirit is not producing power by your thoughts, but by your spoken word. This is the word of God spoken out through your mouth.

Remember, the Ultimate Weapon is Prayer (An Earthly License for Heavenly Interference).

Understand that prayer is a continuous conversation with God and should be made without ceasing (1st Thessalonians 5:16-18). As we grow in our relationship and love for Jesus Christ, we will naturally desire to talk to Him.

CONCLUSION

As we close this first Book in the Trilogy, No other era in the history of the church demands a thorough understanding of spiritual warfare than now. With the advent of COVID 19, the church as it were was almost caught off guard. Our traditional church services approaches were no longer relevant as it was practically impossible to congregate. We at New Beginning Ministries had a Mandate from God NOT TO CLOSE THE DOORS OF THE CHURCH. *(We followed CDC guidelines)* and had in person services and also facebook live services. The church by nature was to play a leading role reassuring the congregations and the community of the hope of salvation and the protection of God as spell out in His promises to us. On the contrary, some church like everyone was also seeking for survival in the face of the legislation that was introduced to curb the spread of COVID 19. We as belivers Ambassadors of Jesus are under Depolmic immunity according to Palms 91 . Looking back at the scriptures, you will observe that the teachings of Jesus Christ were designed to equip the church for a time like ours today. Thus, it has become essential for Belivers to heed the advice of Apostle Paul in putting on the whole armor of God (Ephesians 6:11-18).

This chapter marks the end of the first book in the trilogy and highlights aspects of the next two books titled "The Ultimate Weapon Is Prayer" and "In Him Yes and in Him Amen - The promises of God." The concept of the book Daily Put On The Whole Armor of God "Dress for Spiritual Warfare" in essence, encourages believers to be fully prepared for spiritual battles. It reminds and counsels us on the nature of our warfare. That is, they are not secular or human but spiritual. As a result, our instrument of engagement is strictly spiritual. We also discovered from this teaching that as Christian believers we understand spiritual battles cannot be fought and won using our physical strength or secular military gears as corroborated is the following scriptures.

For we do not wrestle against flesh and blood, but against principalities, against powers, against the rulers of the darkness of this age, against spiritual hosts of wickedness in the heavenly places (Ephesians 6:12)

For the weapons of our warfare are not carnal but mighty in God for pulling down strongholds, casting down arguments and every high thing that exalts itself against the knowledge of God, bringing every thought into captivity to the obedience of Christ, and being ready to punish all disobedience when your obedience is fulfilled (2 Corinthians 10:4-6)

Christian believers are required to be strong in the Lord and in the power of his might (Ephesians 6:10-12). These scriptures are so true in our modern-day. Recognizing that we cannot prevail in spiritual battles with our strength, might, skill, or physical ability (1 Samuel 2:9). But, what the Lord God Almighty can do through His Holy Spirit that dwells in us (Zechariah 4:6).

We are to put on the whole armor of God to be able to withstand the tricks of Satan the enemy. The wiles of the devils are his deceits. The wiles of the devil also mean when he whispers things in your ears that are false and when he sets up event after event to keep you distracted, depressed, and frustrated like the case of Job (Job 1:13-22). As I said earlier these are some of the wiles or craftiness of the devil; we have a responsibility to understand that Apostle Paul referred to them as wiles to let us know they are not unto Death.

The whole armor includes offensive and defensive weapons (Ephesians 6:13-17). Three pieces of armor we have to put on for defense and another three pieces of armor we have to take up for the offensive. Understand the sword of the Holy Spirit, which is the word of God, work as the offensive and defensive weapon. Whereas the word of God one hand as the offensive weapon helps us, to actively and aggressively attack the enemy. On the other hand, the word of God as a defensive weapon helps us to hold off the enemy. This brings us to prayer - the ultimate weapon of our spiritual warfare and the subject of the next book in the trilogy.

Prayers are the only way we win our spiritual battles. Once you have your whole armor on, the ultimate weapon is to be able to pray. The kingdom of heaven can only invade earth through the mechanism of prayer. Consequently, if you cannot pray about your situation God is not obligated to intervene. Prayer is a mandatory and not an optional spiritual weapon. As, believers to win your battles with Satan, you must know how to pray. This is why the disciples asked Jesus Christ to teach them how to pray (Luke 11:1-4). Prayers involve petitioning God about the things you seek as seen in the following scriptures.

Finally, the Results of answered prayers is the promises of God which is the subject of the third book in the trilogy. Prayer helps us to activate the promises of God; it also helps us to know what God's promises are. Through praying, we can receive revelation about the promises of God. Another important role of prayers in knowing the promises of God is that prayers produce strength in your spirit to pursue your divine calling base on the promises of God. When, you pray you are motivated to accomplish God's promises concerning the will of God for our life as Ambassadors of Christ. But, how can one engage prayers to activate the promises of God?

Recognizing the relevance of the promises of God to the church, the third book in the trilogy: In Him Yes and In Him Amen "The promises of God" (2 Corinthians 1:20) was conceived. It reveals how the teaching in the first two book are foundational to receiving the promises of God and clarify the need to understand that your victory as a believer is based in the promises of God.

An inspiration of the Holy Spirit the book educates believers on the promises of God, so, they can take delivery of the full victory in Jesus Christ. The believer is consistently engaged in one battle or the other; this has left so many believers despondent and vulnerable to the enemy. We are full of faith to engage in spiritual warfare. The spiritual ingredient contained in this book will boost your faith in God by recognizing God's promises to you are guaranteed and cannot be stolen but you can be distracted from them. The book also exposes how Satan distracts believers from God's promises right from the creation of Adam and Eve (Genesis 3). That through distraction, he still robs believers of their glorious destiny and heritage in Jesus Christ to this day.

The promises of God are yes and amen. God is the ultimate Promise maker and he is the ultimate promise keeper. The promises of God are yes and amen, why do believers live without the evidence of these promises? If, you are not sure of God's promises and you are not familiar with them, and do not fellowship with them either. Beloved, God's promises are rarely visible in such a life.

God's promises are guaranteed by His word. As believers, your relationship with God is fashioned by your response to His promises. Often, these promises are the answers to despair. They are carriers and assurance of divine provision, protection, safety, and security especially in these trying times of COVID 19. Nonetheless, due to human nature, there is naturally a gap between God's promises to you and receiving these promises; this gap is also visible in praying and receiving the answers to your prayers. The scriptural bridge that closes this gap is Faith in God! (Mark 11:22-24)

So Jesus answered and said to them, "Have faith in God. For assuredly, I say to you, whoever says to this mountain, 'Be removed and be cast into the sea,' and does not doubt in his heart, but believes that those things he says will be done, he will have whatever he says. Therefore I say to you, whatever things you ask

> **when you pray, believe that you receive them, and you will have them. (Mark 11:22-24)**

But, this faith in God works with the promises of God. Recall the scriptures teach faith comes by hearing, and hearing by the word of God (Romans 10:17). It thus behooves the believer to have an accurate knowledge of God's promises. According to google there are 7,487 promises made by God to humankind.

Engaging in spiritual warfare demand you have the accurate knowledge of the scriptures and the promises of God. Consequently, we are in a spiritual battle and engage in constant conflict with the accuser of the brothren, understand the promises that guarantee your victory concerning the battle or success concerning the conflict. Furthermore, when you are petitioning God on a prayer point you have to understand the promises of God concerning what you are praying about. Being armed with the assured promise of God guarantees your victory and success in any battle.

Praise God!

ABOUT THE AUTHOR

Senior Pastor Teresa S. McCurry

SENIOR PASTOR TERESA MCCURRY is an ordained minister of the Gospel of Jesus Christ. She co-labors with her husband, Apostle Gregory McCurry, of New Beginning Ministries (NBM) doing the work of the Lord as a ministry team.

"We introduce a Real God, to Real people with Real issues"

Pastor Tee was called to ministry in 2010 under the leadership of Apostle Leon and Pastor Margie Nelson. She has traveled extensively, educating and inspiring others with her unique approach of conveying information. She has a heart for doing missions work around the world. She was set into the Office of a Prophet and consecrated in 2018.

This was the beginning of a great and powerful deliverance move of God in her life to reach the hurting and lost. God anointed Pastor Tee with spiritual eyesight and ability to speak into people's lives and immediately deliverance takes place to bring forth healing to broken-hearted souls, to proclaim liberty to the captives, and set their hearts completely free.

Pastor Tee is dedicated to helping people who seek to make a positive change.

Her marketplace ministry extends beyond the walls of the church. She is a Beauty Entrepreneur, Inspirational Speaker, International Bible Teacher and International Bestselling Author: she has been a licensed cosmetologist with over 30 years of beauty industry expertise. She holds a Bachelor's degree in Applied Business Administration. Teresa's passion for the beauty industry standards are displayed in the excellence with which she leads by example educating, serving, and beautifying clients while inspiring them to reach their God given purpose.

Teresa's Discipleship is personal and unscripted. She is prophetic in nature and lead by the Holy Spirit. What she offers is leadership training that is personalized to each of her Disciples' unique situations and needs. She works with a limited number of clients each year and she works with them in a few different ways: Personal Discipleship, Signature Group Discipleship Coaching, and PTU ~ Pastor Tee University (coming Soon).

She is currently known as Super Tee Inspires; she chairs Christian Networking Entrepreneurs "CNE" a community outreach of NBM we encourage creative thinking, inspire meaningful dialogue and promote personal and business development through fellowship that will spotlight and support Christian businesses.

Super Tee is the founder of the MCS~Fund whose sole mission is to generate unrestricted funds for Sickle Cell Anemia affected individuals. Through Supportive Services and Advocacy, serving the needs of people plagued by this disease is not only a mission, but also a passion.

Pastor Tee's "honors and awards": she received an honorary doctorate in Humanitarian for having over 20 years of volunteer service to the Sickle cell community from the Global International Alliance By the Authority of the International Association of Christian Counselors.

Pastor Tee also serves on the Board of Directors at Detroit Shoreway Community Development Organization (DSCDO), as Board Secretary and Institutional Representative.

www.ingramcontent.com/pod-product-compliance
Lightning Source LLC
Chambersburg PA
CBHW071224090426
42736CB00014B/2963